Transracial Adoption and Foster Care

Practice Issues for Professionals

Joseph Crumbley

CWLA Press • Washington, DC

CWLA Press is an imprint of the Child Welfare League of America. The Child Welfare League of America (CWLA), the nation's oldest and largest membership-based child welfare organization, is committed to engaging all Americans in promoting the well-being of children and protecting every child from harm.

CHILD WELFARE LEAGUE OF AMERICA, INC.
440 First Street, NW, Third Floor, Washington, DC 20001-2085
E-mail: books@cwla.org

CURRENT PRINTING (last digit)
10 9 8 7 6 5 4 3 2 1

Cover design by Luke Johnson

Printed in the United States of America

ISBN # 0–87868–717-3

Library of Congress Cataloging-in-Publication Data
Crumbley, Joseph.
     Transracial adoption and foster care : practice issues for
  professionals / Joseph Crumbley
        p.   cm.
     Includes bibliographical references (p.).
     ISBN 0-87868-717-3 (alk. paper)
     1. Interracial adoption--United States.   2. Foster home care--
  United States.   3. Family social work--United States.   I. Title.
  HV875.64.C78   1999   99-26148
     362.73'4'0973--dc21   CIP

Contents

Introduction

In *The Bluest Eye*, author Toni Morrison writes about a young Black girl who wishes that her eyes were blue, so she would be as beautiful as all the blond, blue-eyed children in her school:

> Each night, without fail, she prayed for blue eyes. Fervently, for a year she had prayed. Although somewhat discouraged, she was not without hope. To have something as wonderful as that happen would take a long time.
>
> Thrown, in this way, into the binding conviction that only a miracle could relieve her, she would never know her beauty. She would see only what there was to see: the eyes of other people. [Morrison 1994, pp. 46-47]

How devastating to judge your own beauty by the standards of a culture that is not your own! As professionals, our job is to help children and families value and nurture their own unique beauty. This is often a daunting task.

Transracial adoption and foster care has been a controversial topic throughout this decade—a topic that has led to arguments and divisions between families, neighbors, professionals, and politicians on both local and national levels. The purpose of this book is to go beyond the arguments and ask the question: How do we as professionals help children and families make transracial adoptions and foster placements work? How do we help them recognize their beauty?

In 1997, approximately 17% of all domestic adoptions were transracial [DHHS 1999]. These were adoptions in which at least one of the parents' race was different from the child's. In 1996, 11,340 children born outside of the United States were adopted by Americans [U.S. State Department 1998]. The largest number of these children were adopted from China (3,388), Taiwan (3,333), and regions of the former Soviet Union.

As of March 31, 1998, at least 110,000 children are in foster care with the goal of adoption. Twenty-nine percent are white, 59% are African American, and 10% are Latino [DHHS 1999]. Twenty-seven percent (3,601) of the African American children who were adopted and 7% of the white children were in transracial adoptions. The reality of children living in transracial families raises many questions:

- How does a positive racial and/or cultural identity develop?

- What is the impact of transracial adoption and foster care on the child and family?

- What are the special needs of foster or adopted children living in transracial families?

- What are the parenting tasks specific to transracial families?

- What skills, attitudes, knowledge, and resources must parents in transracial families have or develop?

- What training and competencies should professionals have if they are involved or intervening with transracial families?

- What assessment tools and training programs exist for the screening, selection, and preparation of prospective adoptive or foster parents?

- What case management processes are specific to foster or adoptive transracial families?

- What are essential components in effective recruitment programs?

My goal with this book is to provide professionals, agencies, and organizations with information that I have found to be useful in serving foster and adopted children in transracial families, the children's adoptive and foster parents, and families with children who were adopted internationally.

I have divided the book into three parts: the first part describes specific ways that practitioners can work with transracial adoptive and foster families to ensure that children develop positive racial and cultural identities. The second part discusses how practitioners might better serve transracial families. The last part addresses professionals concerns, such as cultural competence and recruitment.

Part I: Introducing Families to Racial and Cultural Issues

The chapters in Part I are designed to help professionals introduce some complex issues to adoptive and foster parents. Chapter 1, "Understanding Racial and Cultural Identity," discusses the concept of identity formation and how power shapes a child's positive identity. The chapter also defines the terms "dominant" and "minority" and emphasizes the importance of recognizing that social interactions within the extended family and the community are essential for the child to develop a positive racial and/or cultural identity.

Chapter 2, "Recognizing the Impact of Transracial Placement," assists the professional in identifying the impact of transracial adoption and foster care on the child by providing illustrations of how children, family members, and communities may respond to transracial placement and what strong emotions lie behind those responses.

Part II: Providing Services to Transracial Families

Chapter 3, "Assessment and Training," reviews several assessment tools and guides that are administered by agency professionals or self-administered by prospective parents, as well as several training programs and curricula for prospective foster and adoptive parents.

Chapter 4, "Preparing Children and Families for Placement," discusses how professionals can effectively prepare children and families for transracial placements and also identifies activities that may help with this transition.

Chapter 5, "Identifying Parenting Tasks and Skills," provides an overview of parenting tasks and a discussion of specific skills and capabilities that parents in transracial families should have. This chapter also provides an explanation of prejudice, discrimination, and racism that parents might use with their children.

Chapter 6, "Case Management," offers an overview of activities related to the child's education, medical/health concerns, community networking, and financial and legal tasks. This chapter then describes a continuum of postfoster placement and adoption services and tasks.

Part III: Professionals Concerns

Chapter 7, "Staff Attitudes and Values," discusses how staff can be better prepared to serve and support transracial foster and adoptive families. The discussion focuses on values, standards, and guidelines that agencies can adopt to facilitate their work.

Chapter 8, "Recruitment," discusses the federal requirement that states develop plans to recruit racially diversified families and identifies barriers to recruitment and strategies to minimizing them. The chapter concludes with a review of techniques that might retain families through the training, selection, and approval phases of the recruitment process.

Chapter 9 provides an overview of future trends in transracial adoptions and foster placements. This chapter also identifies challenges that professionals and agencies face in providing services and meeting the expectations of federal legislation (i.e., IEPA). The chapter concludes with recommendations for research to improve legislation, case management, and practices that have an impact on transracial and transcultural adoptions and foster care.

I have included case studies based on my own experiences throughout the text to illustrate various points. I have also incorporated into the chapters some "myths" about transracial adoption and foster care, as well as appropriate responses. An example is given below, and all myths cited in the text are listed at the end of this Introduction.

> **Myth #1:** The emotional issues of adopted or foster children in transracial placements are no different from children in same-race adoption or foster care.

Myths About Transracial Placements

> **Myth #1:** The emotional issues of adopted or foster children in transracial placements are no different from children in same-race adoption or foster care (p. 7).

> **Myth #2:** Developing racial or cultural identity is not necessary to function as a member of a family or society (p. 9).

> **Myth #3:** You're only fostering or adopting a child, not her racial or cultural heritage (p. 14).

Myth #4: The foster or adoptive family can "be all things" to the child. The child's loss of racial origin and sources of racial identity can be replaced by that of his foster or adoptive family (p. 20).

Myth #5: Anyone can foster or adopt transracially/transculturally. No special resources, capabilities, skills, or knowledge are necessary to parent transracially/transculturally (p. 25).

Myth #6: Knowing about a child's racial/cultural identity and needs are not necessary to consider when deciding to foster or adopt transracially/transculturally. Meeting a child's racial and cultural identity needs should not be a determining factor in deciding to adopt transracially/transculturally. In addition, being able to provide a child a safe and permanent home should be the paramount consideration when prospective parents determine their ability to adopt or foster, whether same race or transracially/transculturally (p. 61).

Myth #7: Children in transracial homes should be raised as if they are the same race and culture of the adoptive or foster family. The child should adapt to the family, not the family to the child. Shared racial identity and culture are necessary for family attachment and bonding (p. 64).

Myth #8: Love is enough. The only thing a transracially adopted or foster child needs is a loving and caring family. Consequently, any emotional issues resulting from being in out-of-home care will be remedied, or may not even occur. In fact, the younger they're adopted or placed (i.e., infancy) the less likely children are to experience these emotional issues (i.e., loss, grief, rejection, etc.) (p. 70).

Myth #9: Blacks do not adopt (p. 94).

Myth #10: African-American communities, professionals, and organizations (such as NABSW) are unapproachable and uncompromising regarding transracial adoptions and foster care and would rather have a child languish in foster care than be adopted (p. 95).

Myth #11: There are not sufficient numbers of same-race homes for African American children (p. 96).

References

Morrison, T. (1970). *The bluest eye.* New York: Plume.

U.S. Department of Health and Human Services, Administration on Children, Youth and Families, Children's Bureau [DHHS]. (1999). *Preliminary AFCARS current estimates report.* Washington, DC: Author.

U.S. Department of State, Immigration and Naturalization. (1998). *Statistics on foreign-born adopted children.* Washington, DC: Author.

Part I

Introducing Families to Racial and Cultural Issues

Chapter One
Understanding Racial and Cultural Identity

Our role as professionals is to help adoptive and foster parents recognize the complexity of transracial placements. While most parents are familiar with the stages of child development, based on their own experiences with children, they are unaware of racial and cultural identity development. Such identity development does not mesh in a tidy way with the universal stages of cognitive, psychological, and emotional development that are clearly tied to the age of the child. Rather, demographic and sociological factors play a strong intervening role regarding perceptions of, and attitudes toward, identity.

Rainbow Kids, an online international adoption publication, offers an overview of how racial and ethnic identity develops, which you can use with parents as a guideline for planning appropriate activities. Note how important social interactions are at each of these stages. (The age ranges are approximate.)

- **Birth–Age 3:** Toddlers become aware of physical race and skin color differences and learn names for specific groups. They do not comprehend the real meanings of these labels and may be puzzled by the use of colors to describe both people and objects.

- **Ages 4–6:** Preschoolers can usually identify their own racial or ethnic group and may place a positive or negative value on their own and other groups. Feelings about groups are acquired by absorbing societal messages from the media, literature, toys, and their surroundings, even in the absence of contact or parent instruction.

- **Ages 7–11:** Latency-age children usually have a firmer understanding of their own racial and ethnic identify and—given the opportunity—will explore what it means to be a member of this group. This can be a prime age for participating in group activities with a cultural or educational focus, as well as a time when role models are especially important.

- **Ages 12–18:** Adolescence is usually made up of early and late stages, but the span is included here because the progression is individualistic. This is a time of exploration, including determining the significance of race, ethnicity, culture, adoption, and examining how these apply to the individual. A teen's past experiences with his or her ethnic group identity are important, as those experiences determines whether his or her identity now is positive, negative, or in transition [Rainbow Kids, no date].

Research indicates that the development of racial or ethnic identity begins with the child conforming to the values of the host culture—in this case, the adoptive or foster family. If the family holds negative stereotypes about the child's minority group, the child will consider herself to be a member of an oppressed group [Lin, no date].

Because racial/cultural identity development is significantly influenced by social circumstances and encounters that may or may not occur at any time during the lifespan, it is essential that adoptive and foster parents understand how they, the extended family (including the birth family), and the community (both same-race and that of the adoptive/foster family) can help a child develop a *positive* racial or cultural identity. Much of that understanding centers on the concept of power.

Power and Identity Formation

Theories on social learning, object relations, and identification are useful in explaining how a child's identity (i.e., racial, religious, ethnic, class, or gender) develops [Bandura 1977]. These theories are also useful in understanding the similarities and differences in the development of identities in children from dominant groups and from minority groups experiencing discrimination.

The **dominant** group has power and control over the distribution of goods, services, rights, privileges, entitlements and status. A **minority** group is subject to the power, control, discretion, and distribution of goods and privileges by another group. A **group** may be identified as individuals who share a specific characteristics; i.e., race, religion, political belief, culture, gender, or physical/mental disorders.

The child from the dominant group begins her identity formation by observing what group is in power and by observing that the members of the group in power are like her (i.e., race, gender, religion). Therefore, the child assumes that she is like the members in that group, has the same rights as members in that group, and will achieve similar accomplishment and power as group members. The ultimate result of the child's identity is a sense of positive self-esteem, confidence, worth, entitlements, and goals.

The minority child's identity formation begins with observing what group is in power, observing that members of his group are not in positions of power and control. The minority child also observes and/or experiences prejudice, discrimination, and exposure to stereotypes. Therefore, the minority child assumes that he is like the members in the minority group, has the same limited rights, can only achieve the same accomplishments, position, and status as similar group members, and that he and members of his minority group are not as good as those in power.

What happens, though, when a child is adopted internationally? What if the child's community in the native home was part of a dominant group—but the child is then adopted into a culture where his or her group is regarded as a minority? Once adoptive and foster parents understand the importance of social power, they will be better able to help their child deal with these challenges.

The obvious results of negative group identities are inferiority complexes (i.e., low self-esteem, poor self-image, lack of confidence, entitlements, worth, or rights). The inferiority is not the result of identifying or being a member of a minority group, but from exposure to discrimination, prejudices, and negative stereotypes about one's minority group. A child from a minority group that is celebrated, held in esteem, or that shares power and control with the dominant group can have an identity that is just as positive as a child from the dominant group. Children from celebrated groups can still feel inferior, however, if they consider being *different* as negative.

Imagine a child developing her own gender identity from TV shows, movies, magazines, and peers. Parents need to screen such information and experiences to help the child develop her identity. This holds true for the development of racial, cultural, and family identities.

To counteract the minority child's formation of negative identities, parents need to communicate important principles, such as the following:

- Members of the child's minority group can also make positive achievements, if they are given equal opportunities.

- The child and his minority group have the same rights and entitlements as members of the dominant group.

- The child and his minority group are as good as any other group.

- Stereotypes, prejudices, and discrimination are wrong.

Parents can also offer the child proof that the prejudices and stereotypes are untrue, so that the child can "see it to believe it." This last task may be the most difficult and challenging to accomplish if the minority child's group is not in a position of power, control, or success in the child's environment. Listed below are some alternatives:

- Expose the child to historic figures and information about her group's accomplishments, capacities, value, and culture.

- Redefine and reframe the child's definition of success, strengths, and accomplishments by not using standards and definitions based on those of the dominant group (i.e., highlight individual accomplishments, family commitment, group survival, spiritual and moral integrity, civil rights activities against discrimination).

- Expose the child to members of his minority group who are in positions of power and control (i.e., films, media).

Special Needs of Transracial Families

Myth #1: The emotional issues of adopted or foster children in transracial placements are no different from children in same-race adoption or foster care.

Response: Adopted or foster children placed transracially experience emotional issues reflected in such questions as, "Who are my parents?" "Why didn't they keep me?" "What is my racial and cultural background and history?" "How and where do I found out about it?" "Do I want it?" "Why didn't my race or country keep me?" or "Can I still fit in?"

The transracially adopted or fostered child experiences losses of family and racial and cultural origins (i.e., loss of prior identity, racial isolation, abandonment, fear of racial rejection). The children in both same-race and transracial placements ask, "Will I be accepted in this home, even if I am from a different (biological) family?" In transracial homes the child might also ask, "Will I be accepted even if I'm from a different race?"

Coping with biological as well as racial differences is the first contrast between children in same-race families from those in transracial homes. The second difference is the dual losses of family and racial/cultural origins. These issues can surface even if transracially fostered or adopted children were placed with their families since birth.

The special needs of children in transracial homes result from the realities of negative stereotypes, prejudices, and discrimination. The Minnesota Department of Human Services' *Assessment Guide for Families Adopting Transracially and Crossculturally* [1990] identified seven basic identity needs of children in transracial homes:

- the need to live in an environment that provides the child with positive experiences with her culture;

- the need to have ongoing relationships with same-race and peer role models;

- the need to live in an environment that provides the child with positive racial and ethnic pride, coping, problemsolving, and survival skills;

- the need to have parent(s) who can help the child acquire experiences and information that develop positive cultural and racial identity;

- the need to have parent(s) who can recognize and empathize with the child's feelings of racial, cultural, and family-of-origin differences from the transracial family;

- the need to have parent(s) who can empathize and understand the child's experience of living in a race-conscious society; and

- the need to have parent(s) who are knowledgeable of their child's dietary, skin, hair, and health care needs.

Following are some recommendations that you might suggest to transracial families about appropriate, supportive environments. The perfect environment, of course, is in communities where members of the child's cultural or racial origin also live. The next alternative is living close to a child's cultural or racial community. This would also allow for same-race contacts, peers, networking, role models, and social involvement. In this setting, the foster or adoptive parents can be involved personally and socially with members of the child's race or culture in a neighborly and more natural context. Consequently, the child's same-race contacts naturally evolve as an extension of his or her foster or adoptive parents' personal relationships, friendships, and involvement in community and social activities.

When geographic proximity is not possible, the parents can be involved with other local cultural and racial communities (i.e., school, camps, day care, churches, social/athletic organizations, holidays/celebrations, family activities). The child's domestic environment should promote positive cultural and racial pride, information, role models, and experiences. Cultural camps are another alternative for children who are not living close to their racial or cultural communities.

Empathy for and recognition of the child's racial differences and experiences begins with validating the child's recognition of differences in physical appearance, culture, and social treatment. Preparing and equipping the child with skills to cope with differential treatment or reaction by others because of the child's race, culture, or transracial family requires the parents' recognition of the child's cultural or racial differences.

Developing the child's value, self-esteem, and pride in her race and culture begins with the child feeling that her differences are important and valued by her foster or adoptive parents. Parents can communicate this by addressing the child's unique dietary, skin, hair, and health care needs.

> **Myth #2:** Developing racial or cultural identity is not necessary to function as a member of a family or society.

> **Response:** A transracially/transculturally adopted or fostered child will need to develop a positive racial identity to function and cope in a prejudiced and race-conscious society that discriminates. The child is a member of a racial or cultural group that is experiencing prejudice, discrimination, or negative stereotypes.

> The child will also need a positive racial identity to counteract the negative experiences and to maintain her self-esteem. In addition, the child's development and feeling of positive racial identity begins by building and acknowledging her racial identity in her family. Only then will the child will feel positive about herself outside the home and in society.

Conclusion

In summary, you should help foster and adoptive parents understand the following points about children from a minority group or another country who experience prejudice, discrimination, or feeling negatives about "being different":

- These children can develop a negative racial or cultural identity through personal perceptions, experiences, and/or observations (i.e., community, school, or media).

- These children require monitoring, and parents must pay attention to a child's perception of her own racial identity to counteract any sense of inferiority.

- These children should not be expected to develop independently an adequate and positive racial or cultural identity without the positive support and reinforcements from family, role models, and the community.

References

Andojo, E. (1988). Ethnic identity of transethicnally adopted Hispanic adolescents. *Social Work, 33*, 531-35

Bardura, A. (1977). *Social learning theory.* Englewood Cliffs, NJ: Prentice Hall, Inc.

Brenner, E. M. (1993). Identity formation in transracially adopted adolescents. Ph.D. dissertation. California School of Professional Psychology at Berkeley/Alameda.

Cole, J. (1992). *Perceptions of ethnicity identity among Korean-born adoptees and their white-American parents.* Ph.D. dissertation, Columbia University.

Descoteaux, B. C. (1994). Stress and social support experienced by transcultural families. Ed.D. dissertation, University of Rochester.

Dore, E. D. (1995). Identifying similarities and differences among young adolescents who have been adopted: A set of case studies. Ph.D. dissertation, University of Northern Colorado.

Feigelman, W., & Silverman, A. (1984). The long-term effects of transracial adoption. *Social Service Review, 58*, 588-602.

Flores de Kistler, M. J. (1995). The transcultural adoption experience. Ph.D. dissertation, California State University, Long Beach, CA.

Johnson, P., Shireman, J., & Watson, K. [1987] Transracial adoption and the development of Black identity at age eight. *Child Welfare, 66*(1), 45-56.

Lin, J. (no date). *Helping your child develop a positive racial/ ethnic identity.* Available online at http:// www.pactadopt.org/ press/articles/helping.html].

Lydens. (1988). A longitudinal study of cross-cultural adoption: Identity development among Asian at adolescence and early adulthood. Ph.D. dissertation, Northwestern University.

McRoy, R., & Zurcher, L. (1983). *Transracial and inracial adoptees: The adolescent years.* Springfield, IL: Charles C. Thomas Publisher.

McRoy, R., Zurcher, L., & Lauderdale, M. (1984). The identity of transracial adoptees. *Social Casework, 65*, 34-9.

Minnesota Department of Human Services. (1990). Worker's assessment guide for families adopting cross-racially/cross-culturally. St. Paul, MN: Author.

Mortland, C. A., & Egan, M. G. (1997). Vietnamese youth in American foster care. *Social Work, 32*, 240-5.

Rainbow Kids. (no date). *Understanding race and adoption.* Available online on http://www.rainbowkids.com/ 199agesandstages.html].

Scarr, S., & Weinberg, R. (1983). The Minnesota Adoption Studies: Genetic differences and malleability. *Child Development, 54*, 260-7.

Shireman, J. F. (1988). *Growing up adopted: An examination of major issues.* Chicago: Chicago Care Society.

Trolley, B. C., Wallin, J., & Hansen, J. (1995). International adoption: Issues of acknowledgment of adoption and birth culture. *Child and Adolescent Social Work Journal 12*, 465-79.

Vroegh, K. S. (1997). Transracial adoptees: Developmental status After 17 years. *American Journal of Orthopsychiatry, 67*, 568-75.

Chapter Two
Recognizing the Impact of Transracial Placement

As practitioners, you can help parents recognize the impact of transracial placement on the child, as well as the influences that transracial adoption and foster care may have on the child's relationships with the family (adoptive and birth), the extended family, and with the community. This chapter describes typical emotional reactions that children will have and presents some sample questions that children in transracial placements may ask about their racial/ethnic identity. Also included are discussions of how important relationships may be affected, as well as recommendations on how parents can address relationship concerns.

Emotional Reactions

The impact of transracial placements on children may clearly be seen in their emotional reactions. Feeling different from children who live with their birth parents and also from children living with foster or adoptive parents of the same race can prompt **low self-esteem** in the child, especially if he interprets "difference" as "bad or negative." This type of internalization can also result in feelings of rejection and abandonment: "Something's wrong with me. That's why no one wants me."

Inferiority complexes occur when the child stigmatizes being from a race different from his foster or adoptive family. It is common for a child in out-of-home care to say, "I wish you were my parent" or "I wish I looked like you." Such statements are often indicative of the child's attachment to his foster or adoptive family and are based on the child's devaluing his own physical or racial background, or his family of origin. Children, in general, can begin to recognize racial differences as early as 3 years old and can associate stigma with race as early as 6 years old [Clark & Clark 1958].

Children in transracial families are predisposed to address adoption and foster care issues at an early age [Vroegh 1997]. Sometimes the child may want to deny her biological difference or the importance of her differences from foster or adoptive parents to avoid feelings of loss or fantasies. This denial can also happen in transracial families in the form of **racial denial**, which occurs when a child attempts to minimize his racial as well as his biological differences from the foster or adoptive family.

> **Myth #3:** You're fostering or adopting a child, not her racial or cultural heritage.

> **Response:** When you foster or adopt a child transracially, you are also bringing her issues and questions about her race and family to your home. As in same-race adoptions or placements, *not* to question, acknowledge, or discuss with the child her racial difference, history, culture, and origin is to imply that it is wrong to bring up the topics or that the topics are too threatening or not important enough to discuss. Low self-esteem, inferiority, and suppression or denial of identity may be unintended outcomes of such denial.

If a child suddenly or with little preparation has contact with his racial or cultural origin, that encounter may result in **culture shock** (similar to the surprise or shock an adopted child may experience when contacting the birth family). Even with preparation, the child's first contact with a member of her own race or family can be surprising, awkward, and unfamiliar.

The **conflict** in choosing between racial identities and cultures can create a crisis for the child in a transracial family. The biracial child might experience stress from considering the advantages and disadvantages of choosing a particular racial identity. The biracial child may also feel the crisis from being forced to accept only one "assigned" identity when she is biracial or unsure of her biracial origins.

A crisis may also occur when the child feels that he is being disloyal when choosing, searching, or pursuing a racial or cultural identity different from his adoptive or foster family. These feelings and dynamics are analogous to a foster or adopted child pursuing, finding, and identifying with her family of origin. Even with the foster or adoptive family's support, the child may still feel disloyalty issues. See Case Study #1, below.

Case Study #1

This case study is an example of how parents can minimize the cultural crisis and dual loyalties that adopted or foster children can experience in transracial families.

Two adopted African American siblings were attending a family therapy session. Prior to the session, the two adolescent boys met separately with the therapist while waiting for their adoptive parents to arrive. While with the therapist, the boys discussed the Rodney King incident (a videotape of an African American being beaten by white police). The boys were angry and accused the police officers of being prejudiced, racist, and unfair. They talked about what should be done to the officers. Their (white) adoptive parents arrived and entered the session. Both boys immediately discontinued speaking and became silent.

The therapist mentioned to the parents that the boys were discussing the Rodney King incident. Neither the boys or their parents, however, would continue the conversation. In subsequent separate sessions with the siblings, the therapist asked the boys why they didn't continue discussing Rodney King in front of their parents. They're response was, "We don't want to hurt our parents' feelings, and we don't talk about things like that with our parents or other white people."

The therapist shared these comments with the adoptive parents. In the next family meeting, the therapist mentioned his observations while the boys and parents were together. The boys remained silent; however, the parents told the boys that they should be upset about the Rodney King incident and should not be tolerant of anyone, Black or white, who is prejudiced or discriminating. The parents encouraged the boys to be involved as African Americans in protecting the civil rights of their community.

Several weeks later, a white truck driver was filmed being pulled out of his truck and beaten by young African Americans. In the subsequent family sessions, the boys were able to discuss with their parents how prejudice and discrimination affect both "Blacks and whites alike." The adoptive parents were able to validate the siblings' feelings about prejudice and discrimination, give the boys permission and support to have an opinion and take a position, and identify how the boys could be active and committed to their community's development and civil rights.

The Child's Relationship with the Family

Listed below are some typical children's responses that may arise as a result of transracial placement, as well as questions that a child may ask.

Developing and **taking the risk to trust** is a crucial issue for foster or adopted children in both same-race or transracial families.

"Can I trust this family to accept me even if I'm not a member of their (birth) family?"

"Can I trust them to accept me, even if I'm not a member of their race?"

The issue of **racial acceptance or rejection** is implicit in the previous questions. Subsequent questions might be

"Will they accept my family history, origin, and background?"

"Will they accept or reject my racial background and culture?" (i.e., food, music, language, nationality, dress, friends, or search for identity)

The issues of **loyalty and commitment** are reflected in such questions as

"Will they be loyal to me, even if I'm from a different family?"

"Will they be loyal to me and willing to confront members of their own race or family in protection of my rights?"

Concerns about **equal rights and privileges** may be reflected in such questions as

"Will I have the same rights and privileges as others if I'm from a different family, country, or race?"

"Does this family feel that members from my race have the same rights as people in their race?"

Questions about **justice and fairness** might be

"Will this family be fair or not take sides against me even if I'm not a member of their family or race?"

"Will this family's opinions or trust in me be based on getting to know me or what they've heard about foster children, adopted children, or children from my country or race?"

The child may also questions the parents' **motivation** to foster or adopt.

"Did they become adoptive or foster parents for the money?"

"Are they trying to rescue me from my family, country, or my race?"

"Are they trying to show they're cool (liberals) by raising a child that's not theirs or from a different country or race?"

"Are they looking for appreciation or a pat on the back for taking a child unable to be cared for by members of their family, country or race?"

The Child's Relationship to the Community

Practitioners will want to discuss with the child and the family issues that apply to both the racial/cultural communities of the child and of her adoptive or foster families. The child may ask the following question about **trust** in his own racial community:

"Will my community trust my identification with them, even if I am a member of a transracial family?"

In her adopted or foster parents' community (i.e., school, church, stores) the question may be

"Can I trust this community to be nonprejudicial or nondiscriminating even though I'm from a different country or race?"

The child may explore issues of **loyalty** in his own community by asking

"Will my community accept my loyalty and give their loyalty to me even if I'm being raised transracially?"

In his parents' community, a question about loyalty could be

• "Can this community accept my loyalty and give me its loyalty, even if I'm from a different country or race?"

Typical questions about **rejection and acceptance** are

"Will my foster/adopted family and I be rejected in my parent's community because I'm from a different race, or will we be rejected in my community because my adoptive or foster family is from a different race?"

Embarrassment and isolation are raised in such questions as

"Will we be stared at and treated different in my own or my parents' community because we are a transracial family?"

Displacement is an additional issue with which the biracial child must cope. The simple but overwhelming question they might ask is

"In what racial community do I fit, belong, feel accepted, not embarrassed, or isolated?"

Impact on Families

Professionals will need to assist the family as they acknowledge and confront personal and institutional racism, prejudice, and discrimination. Have the family begin with an inventory of personal or family attitudes and feelings about people who are different (i.e., age, gender, sex, class, physical challenges). Family members can also examine their own ideas of how prejudice, discrimination, and superiority and inferiority complexes are developed and eradicated. Finally, family members can be guided as they determine their own personal commitment to confront people who are prejudiced, discriminating, or racist on behalf of their adopted or foster child.

> **Myth #4:** The foster or adoptive family can "be all things" to the child. The child's loss of racial origin and sources of racial identity can be replaced by that of his foster or adoptive family.

> **Response:** Such issues as past memories, attachments, and loyalties may obstruct any foster or adopted child's ability to accept an adoptive or foster family as his source of family identity. This finding also occurs in transracial homes where the child finds it difficult to accept the family's racial origin as his source of racial identity. In fact, the child's losses and void can become more intense than children in same-race adoptions or placement experience. This intensity is due not only to feeling different from children living with birth parent, but also different from (birth, adopted, or foster) children living with families of their race.

Changes in the racial configuration of the family from a single-race family to a biracial or multiracial family is an obvious outcome of adopting or fostering transracially. These changes are often accompanied by changes in society's perception of the family. The family may be viewed as an interracial and/or minority family. Consequently, the family may face a **double jeopardy** of prejudice and discrimination from their own and the child's racial groups. Possible reactions and questions from the adoptive or foster parents' relatives and friends might be

> "How could you adopt or foster a child who is not only *not* from your family, but also not from your race? They may grow up thinking they can marry one of us, or think they're as good as us."

Members from the child's racial group may ask

"What makes you think you can raise that child, when you're not of our race?"

"How dare you?" (a quote to a foster parent from members of their foster child's racial group)

Questions about **competency** may come not only from friends, family, and the community, but also from the foster or adopted child as well. Adoptive and foster parents may sense rejection and feelings of betrayal from their birth children in such questions as

"Weren't we enough to make you happy or feel loved?"

"You not only brought in a stranger from a different family, but also from a different race!" (a quote to an adoptive parent from their birth child)

Embarrassment may also impact family members of the adoptive or foster parents. One birth child commented, "I may have to fight for him if someone calls him a (racial) name, and he's not even my real brother or from the same race." A grandmother stated, "How will I explain where this biracial child came from? People may think you (her daughter) had him." Implicit in the grandmother's statements was that people might assume her daughter had a child from an interracial relationship.

References

Clark, K. B., & Clark, M. P. (1958). Racial identification and preference in Negro children. In E. E. Macoby, T. M. Newcombe, & E. Hartley (Eds.), *Education and psychological measurements* (pp. 89-97). New York, NY: Rinehart and Winston.

Vroegh, K. S. (1997). Transracial adoptees: Developmental status After 17 years. *American Journal of Orthopsychiatry, 67*, 568-75.

Part II

Providing Services to Transracial Families

Chapter Three
Assessment and Training

One way that we as practitioners can fully support transracial placement is to ensure that we use appropriate methods of assessing and training families. This chapter reviews several existing tools and curricula designed to address the specific needs of such placements.

> **Myth #5:** Anyone can foster or adopt transracially/transculturally. No special resources, capabilities, skills, or knowledge are necessary to parent transracially/transculturally.

> **Response:** Specialized recruitment, assessment, and training of families for transracial/transcultural adoption or out-of-home care is essential, because the child will need to address the losses of racial, cultural, and family-of-origin identity, and to cope with social and familial acceptance of his birth status (as an adopted or foster child) and racial origin. Helping the child address these issues requires special families with specialized knowledge, resources, skills, and capabilities.

Assessment Tools

The assessment tools reviewed in this chapter have several desired goals, including the following:

- To evaluate the parents' knowledge of issues, parenting skills, tasks, capabilities, and resources needed to parent a child of a different race or culture;

- To determine a parent's current readiness to adopt transracially; and

- To determine what additional skills, knowledge, or resources will be necessary for the individual to become competent in parenting a child of a different race or culture.

Assessment tools can either be agency- or self-administered. I strongly recommend that self-assessment tools be used if confidentiality is necessary for the user to honestly and accurately complete the assessment, if the user is part of a self-selection or self-elimination process, or if anonymity is necessary for the agency or individual considering transracial/cultural adoption or foster care

Agency-administered assessment tools would be appropriate if your agency is developing training and education programs to enhance the parents' strengths and limits. These tools are also useful when pre- and postevaluation are needed to determine the effectiveness of training and changes in the parents' knowledge, attitudes, and skills and if you need information about the parents' competence as part of a screening, elimination, certification, training orientation, or licensing process. Agency-administered assessments are also necessary if parents need assistance in completing the assessment because of physical, language, or educational challenges.

The areas for evaluation should include the following:

- Personal motivations for adopting or fostering in general, and transracially/transculturally, specifically;

- Personal awareness of attitudes and values toward other racial groups and cultures and perceptions of racism, prejudice, and discrimination;

- The parents' understanding of the importance of their role in the formation of the child's racial/cultural identity and an awareness of how their own identities were developed;

- The racial and cultural configuration and composition of the parents' community regarding racial/cultural integration and same-race contacts, experiences, and relationships for the child;

- The parents' lifestyle regarding the integration and incorporation of multicultural traditions in their home, as well as exposure and interaction with different cultural and racial communities and friends;

- Parenting styles, networks, and resources that develop positive personal, racial, and cultural identities and that teach survival skills and address the health and cosmetic needs of the child; and

- Knowledge and awareness of how transracial or transcultural parenting will impact them, their children and friends, and the foster or adopted child's extended family.

I strongly recommend that agencies or organizations using assessment instrument have their staff experience what it is like to be evaluated with the tool. Staff then become more familiar with the material and more sensitive to the participants' reactions to the assessment process. The following sections describe some effective assessment tools.

Self-Awareness Tool

The *Self-Awareness Tool* was developed by the North American Council on Adoptable Children's Transracial Parenting Project to provide parents "an opportunity—in the confidentiality of their own home—to determine if fostering or adopting children of another race or culture is appropriate for their family" [Bower 1998a]. The tool also helps parents understand the experiences and feelings they will encounter when parenting a child of a different race or culture. The ultimate goal of the tool is to provide parents with information that allows them to make an informed decision about fostering or adopting transracially and to self-evaluate their "personal capabilities or potential" to adequately parent a child from a different race or culture. (See Appendix A for an excerpt.)

The *Self-Awareness Tool* engages parents in a personal evaluation of nine categories: personal motivation, personal values, home, cultural exposure, family, relationships, community, cultural identity, and race. Questions are presented through true-life scenarios related by children and parents from transracial or transcultural families (i.e., African American, Native American, Latino, white, and Asian American, both domestic and international). After reading the scenarios, the reader answers the questions, completes an exercise, and provides feedback and information about the topic, exercise, and questions in a written discussion. This format is repeated with each of the nine categories.

The final section of the tool is a self-assessment of parents' capabilities, potentials, strengths, and limits based on their responses in the nine categories. The parents then determine their readiness to foster or adopt transracially. In the conclusion section of the tool, the Council states, "It is better to decide NOT to raise a child of a different race or culture than to try and fail" [Bower 1998a].

Multiethnic Parenting Assessment Guide

The Connecticut Department of Children and Family Services developed the *Multiethnic Parenting Assessment Guide* [Closs et al. 1995] for social workers to use in assessing the parenting capability of families who desire to adopt or foster transracially or transculturally.

The guide numerically rates the prospective parents in four primary areas: race and heritage, motivation and support systems, community opportunities for the child to have same-race or same-culture role models and peer relations, and lifestyle and parenting ability. The interviewer gathers information through close- and open-ended questions. The responses are categorized on a graduated scale from low to high scores.

- **Race and heritage.** The parents are rated on three factors: their self-identity and awareness, cultural exploration, and their prospective on race and discrimination.

- **Motivation and support.** The parents are rated on their reason to parent transracially or transculturally, how they decided on the child's racial or cultural origin, and on the parent's description of their qualifications to adopted or foster transracially or transculturally. The parents are also evaluated on their discussion of the impact and reaction to their decision by family, friends, extended family, and neighbors, and on the current level of interaction they have with the prospective child's racial or ethnic group and community.

- **Community opportunities for the child to have same-race relationships.** This section rates the racial composition of the parents' community (i.e., churches, neighborhood, daycare, schools) and access to the child's community and members of his racial or cultural group.

- **Lifestyles and parenting factors.** Parents are evaluated on their ability to teach the child skills in managing racial and social issues (i.e., prejudice or discrimination); to develop the child's racial and cultural identity; to address the child's dietary and cosmetic, hair, and skin care; and to incorporate the child's culture and traditions into the family.

Workers' Assessment Guide for Families Adopting Cross-Racially/Cross-Culturally

The Minnesota Department of Human Services developed the *Worker's Assessment Guide for Families Adopting Cross-Racially/ Cross-Culturally* [MDHS 1990] to be administered by social workers to prospective parents who desire to adopt transracially. Information is gathered through close- and open-ended questions and parent experiential tasks.

The purpose of the guide is to "assess an applicant's capacity and ability to meet the unique identity needs of children" in transracial/transcultural adoptions. The guide provides a list of identity needs specific to a child who has been adopted transracially or transculturally. (The identity needs appear to apply primarily to domestic adoptions. Some issues, however, are applicable to domestic and out-of-country adoptees.) The interviewer also rates the "desirable" capabilities a parent should possess to meet the identity needs of a child adopted "cross-racially/culturally." The categories for assessment include

- experiences and understanding regarding the role of race and heritage,

- motivation and support,

- a community providing opportunities for same-race role models and peer relationships, and

- lifestyle and parenting abilities.

In addition to being interviewed about these categories, parents are also assigned tasks. Under the category of racial experiences and heritage, the parent is asked to attend a community meeting, social event, church, or to engage in activities in the child's racial or cultural community of origin. The interviewer then discusses with the applicant her or his feelings of being a minority or "the only one."

The interviewer provides conclusions and recommendations about the parenting capabilities in a structured written format that includes

- strengths and weakness by category,

- whether deficiencies can be corrected and how,

- how deficiencies can affect the child in both the long- and short-term, and

- how the applicant responded to tasks and opportunities to correct deficiencies.

Case Study #2

This case study is an example of assessing a prospective adoptive parents' ability to address the racial and identity needs of a biracial child. This assessment highlights the strengths and limits of the prospective parents, risk factors to the child if racial and identity needs are not addressed, and the capabilities, resources, and skills parents will need in order to address a biracial child's racial and cultural issues. Case Study #6 is a subsequent assessment of the same foster family nine months later, highlighting the parents' preparation, acquisitions of skills and resources to be considered for a home study, and later adopt their foster child.

Evaluation and Recommendation for Home Study

Foster child: James, 2 years old, biracial (African American and white)

Foster parents: Mr. and Mrs. T, white

Present at evaluation: child and parents together

Reason for Referral

CYS has requested a family evaluation of James and his foster parents to assess the attachment between James and his foster parents, and to determine Mr. and Mrs. T's ability to parent a biracial child.

This evaluation will be used to determine whether the T family should be considered for a home study, in response to their request and interest in adopting James.

Background Information

James is 2 years old and has been residing with the T family since he was 2 months old. His birth mother is white and birth father is Black. Parental rights were recently terminated. Following the termination of rights, Mr. and Mrs. T expressed an interest to CYS in adopting James.

Mr. and Mrs. T are white and have been married 27 years. They reside in a predominantly white community. They have been birth parents to three children, ages 26, 22, and 21, and grandparents to five children, who Mrs. T now baby-sits on a daily basis, Monday through Friday.

Mr. T described himself as peripheral and not very involved in raising his natural children, due to his occupation as a long-distance truck operator/owner for 27 years.

Since the children's marriages, Mrs. T has devoted most of her time to baby-sitting her grandchildren (ages 5, 4, 3, 2 1/2 years, and 20 months old), as well as being a foster parent for three years. Mr. T is no longer on the road and has been employed locally for the past two years. Mr. T feels that this time with his grandchildren and being a foster parent has given him the opportunity to enjoy the parenthood he missed with his own children.

Mr. and Mrs. T have provided foster care to six children, ranging in ages from 2 months to 2 1/2 years and of white and Black races.

James is reported to have negotiated normal physical and developmental milestones appropriate for his age. His social and emotional development in the areas of impulse control, attention span, accepting limits, and socialization skills also appear appropriate.

Child's Attachment and Readiness for Adoption

James is personally attached and bonded with his foster parents. Although James was unable to adequately verbalize his feelings, he and his parents' attachment was evidenced by

- their open display of rituals and routines in exchanging affection;

- James' expectation and acceptance of comforting when feeling unsafe and unsure in a strange environment (i.e., my office);

- the parents' description of consistent structure and routines around play, dining, bedtime, and leisure time that denotes a safe, secure, and nurturing environment; and

- nonverbal communication between the parents and James of limits, expectations, and positive reinforcements during the interview (i.e., managing his restlessness, limiting his curiosity to touch, giving James positive reinforcement for appropriate behavior).

James is able to differentiate, separate, and appropriately attach to significant others as demonstrated by his attachment to Mr. and Mrs. T. James would experience typical separation anxiety if removed from Mr. and Mrs. T's home. Since James' ability to attach is within normal ranges, he should be able to bond with different or adoptive parents, if properly prepared for adoption.

Parents' Readiness to Adopt a Biracial Child

Mr. and Mrs. T have approximately three years' experience as foster parents and raised three birth children to adulthood.

When asked if and how race had an impact on developing a child's self-esteem and identity, Mr. and Mrs. T answered, "No impact." When asked if and how race affected their self-esteem and identity throughout their childhood, they answered, "No effect." However, when asked if being proud of and knowledgeable of their race, culture, and heritage enhanced their self-identity, image, and esteem, they did answer, "Yes." Mr. and Mrs. T acknowledged the impact of race on a child's development, but also indicated that race was not necessary in the development of a child's personality and identity.

When asked if addressing racial issues was necessary in raising a biracial child, Mr. and Mrs. T answered, "No." When asked if they would inform their biracial foster child about discrimination he would encounter, they stated that they would "deal with it when it occurs, rather than creating problems or situations that may not occur." When asked if they would prepare the child with ways of responding to discrimination or prejudices, their response was again to "wait until it happened, rather than create anxiety or a defensive attitude in the child." When asked if they would network with Black families, communities, or activities that would expose their child to positive role models and heritage, Mr. and Mrs. T stated that they did not have any Black friends and told the CYS adoption supervisor that they wouldn't "manufacture" Black friends. However, they would network with Black organizations and investigate the possibility of membership in a local integrated Baptist church and local schools.

Summary and Recommendations

Mr. and Mrs. T are quite competent in providing a protective, stimulating, and nurturing environment for an adopted child of the same race. At present, however, they would not be able to provide the parenting and socialization necessary to prepare a biracial child for discrimination and prejudice.

Their inability is due to not feeling a need to prepare or inform the child about the types and forms of discrimination and prejudice, not providing the child with a repertoire of responses necessary in coping with racial inequities and prejudices, not having the interracial network and associations to provide the child with positive Black or biracial role models to counteract negative stereotypes, and not feeling it necessary to address racial issues in developing a child's self-esteem, image, identity, and personality. Consequently, as a biracial child, James is at risk of the following:

- Developing a poor self-image and low self-esteem, due to society's projection of negative stereotypes and limited exposure to positive Black or biracial role models;

- Being emotionally vulnerable to unanticipated racial discrimination and prejudice;

- Feelings of alienation from Black or biracial people and communities because of primary exposure to white communities and alienation from white communities when unexpectedly confronted with discrimination from peers; and

- Being unaware of coping skills and alternative responses to discrimination other than responding angrily, irrationally, and destructively toward self or others.

Case Study #3

This case study is an example of how assessments can be used in identifying a prospective adoptive parents' strengths and limits and how assessments can be used in the education and preparation of families for transracial adoptions. (This is a nine-month follow-up to Case Study #2.)

Evaluation and Recommendation for Home Study

Foster child: James, 2 years old, biracial (African American and white)

Foster parents: Mr. and Mrs. T, white

Present at evaluation: child and parents together

Assessment instrument: *Workers' Assessment Guide for Families Adopting Cross-Racially/Cross-Culturally* by Minnesota Department of Human Services and Department of Health and Human Services

Date of Evaluation: Nine months after first evaluation (see Case Study #2)

Reason for Evaluation

The purpose of the second evaluation was to determine if Mr. and Mrs. T could address the racial identity issues of a biracial child as adoptive parents. This evaluation will be used to determine whether the T family should be considered for a home study, in response to their request to adopt their foster child, James.

In the initial evaluation, Mr. and Mrs. T were determined to be quite competent in providing a protective, stimulating and nurturing environment for an adopted child. However, at that time, they were also determined unable to address the identity issues of a biracial child. Their inability was due to

- not feeling it necessary to address racial issues in developing a biracial child's self-esteem, image, and identity;

- not feeling a need to inform or prepare the child for the types and forms of discrimination and prejudices;

- not feeling required to provide the child with a repertoire of responses necessary in coping with racial prejudices and inequities; and

- not having the interracial network necessary for providing the child positive Black and biracial role models to counteract negative stereotypes.

The first objective of this evaluation was to determine if Mr. and Mrs. T felt it was necessary to address the racial identity issues of a biracial child. In their previous evaluation, they felt addressing racial identity was unnecessary. Mr. and Mrs. T were also unable to fully comprehend how racial identity impact self-image and self-esteem.

When asked about the importance of racial identity during this evaluation, Mr. and Mrs. T stated that ethnic and racial identity was necessary in developing anyone's self-identity and self-esteem. When asked why, they further stated that pride and knowledge about one's ethnic or racial culture, heritage, history, and accomplishments gives a person a sense of personal pride, positive self-esteem, and identity. They also felt that biracial children need positive racial identity to counteract the negative racial identities and stereotypes encountered in society, to develop positive self-esteem, and to avoid developing inferiority complexes.

When asked how they would help develop positive racial identity, Mr. and Mrs. T referred to methods they were already instituting in their family. Their methods included personal interaction with Black, white, and biracial families; education about his biracial background and history; and modeling and incorporating as parents a multicultural lifestyle (i.e., toys, food, music, art, literature, grooming, and cosmetics).

Mr. and Mrs. T acknowledged a lack of appreciation for the importance of racial identity in developing their own self-esteem and identity in the first evaluation. They attributed their current awareness to personal education and participation in multiracial sensitivity group for birth and adoptive parents during the past nine months.

The second objective of this evaluation was to determine if Mr. and Mrs. T considered it necessary to educate or prepare a biracial child for prejudice and discrimination. In their first evaluation, the couple felt it was not necessary to address prejudice and discrimination with James in advance. In fact, their approach was to "wait until it happens."

They now feel that is essential to prepare James or any child for prejudice and discrimination to minimize trauma to the child (i.e., shock, disillusionment, inferiority) and teach the child controlled, rather than reactive responses.

When asked how they would educate and prepare James, they stated that they would explain how and why Blacks and other minorities are discriminated against; provide James with a repertoire of responses to discrimination (i.e., legal community and individual); and be prepared to confront racism, prejudice, and discrimination, in general and on behalf of James, specifically. Mr. and Mrs. T felt that they still needed education in how racism, prejudice, and discrimination are evidenced (overt and covert/institutional and personal), and techniques of responding (reactive vs. proactive).

The evaluation's third objective was to determine if Mr. and Mrs. T felt it was necessary to have James interact with Black, white, and biracial families and communities. Prior to their initial evaluation, they expressed to a CYS adoption supervisor their reluctance to "manufacture" friends for James. During their initial evaluation, they reconsidered their reluctance and stated their willingness to do "whatever was in James' best interest." However, they admitted not having either the network or the social friends with whom James could interact.

During this evaluation, Mr. and Mrs. T were able to explain why networking was in James' "best interest." They felt it was necessary to counteract negative stereotypes through James' personal contact with positive role models, and minimize James' alienation or estrangement from white, Black, or biracial communities by having multiracial experiences.

When asked how they would access multiple cultures and communities, they identified several strategies:

- continued membership in their multiracial organization for adoptive families;

- participation in multiethnic conferences and sensitivity groups;

- use of multiracial, ethnic play, and educational toys and books with James;

- development of a network of personal multiracial friends; and

- identification of daycare and schools that are integrated and have multiethnic curriculums and staff.

Mr. and Mrs. T felt compelled during this evaluation to network and interact with Black, white, and biracial families and communities, to provide James with positive role models that counteract negative stereotypes and minimize alienation from white, Black, or biracial communities. They reported identifying integrated daycare programs and schools, interacting with personal friends of multiracial backgrounds, and becoming members of a multiethnic support group for biracial and adoptive families.

In summary, I would recommend that Mr. and Mrs., T be considered for a home study, based on their ability to address the racial identity issues of their foster child, James. This recommendation is contingent upon Mr. and Mrs. T's continued involvement with multiracial educational and sensitivity groups and ongoing involvement in postadoptive therapy for parents with biracial children. Therapy will need to be long-term and periodic, in keeping with the adoption and developmental issues James and his adoptive parents will encounter (i.e., toddler, during latency, adolescent, and as a young adult).

Struggle for Identify

The video, "Struggle for Identity: Issues in Transracial Adoptions," interviews adult adoptees and a few adoptive parents from transracial/transcultural families, who discuss a variety of issues:

- feeling different in their adoptive family, community, and community of racial origin;

- how they developed identities;

- coping and survival skills they needed as adoptees of color; and

- how they viewed their adoptive parents' motivation and readiness to adopt them.

The adoptive parents discuss changes in the family's racial identity, how the family became multiracial, their role in developing the child's identity, and sources of support, education, and mentoring to the parents from the child's community of origin.

This video would be useful in a discussion with prospective foster and adoptive parents for assessing their sensitivity and awareness of transracial/transcultural issues and their preparedness to foster or adopt transracially [New York State Citizen's Coalition for Children 1998].

Below the Surface

Pact: An Adoption Alliance has developed a self-assessment guide, *Below the Surface,* for adoptive families considering transracial/transcultural adoptions domestically or internationally [Hall & Steinberg 1998]. The goals of the guide are to provide prospective parents with measures to assess their comfort with transracial/transcultural issues and with information that will be more useful to increasing their ability to parent transracially/culturally. (See Appendix B for an excerpt.) The guide assesses personality, attitude, lifestyle, and knowledge.

- **Personality.** This category helps the parents evaluate their emotional and behavioral "tendencies and temperament" when encountering situations common to transracial/transcultural families.

- **Attitudes.** The category assists parents in becoming aware of their feelings, biases, and assumptions about adoption and race.

- **Lifestyle.** This section assesses the compatibility of the parents' environment (i.e., friends, neighbors, family, schools, church, child care) with the adopted child's racial or cultural identity and needs.

- **Knowledge.** This section measures the parent's awareness of the adopted child's heritage, diet, skin/hair care, development of racial identity, and the history of other cultural groups.

The parent answers multiple-choice questions under each category. The possible answers to each question are numerically weighted, rated, and totaled by category. The categorical scores are then totaled to measure the individual's overall suitability to parent. In addition to measuring a parent's suitability, the guide also provides information about the strength or limits the individual has or needs to address to adopt transracially or transculturally. The final section of the guide provides a guide for analyzing the diversity of the parents' present associates, friends, and activities.

Parent Training Programs

In general, parent training material should help parents understand the special needs of children in transracial or transcultural families; prepare parents for the impact on how transracial/cultural adoptions or placements impact them, their family, and the child; equip parents with the skills, knowledge, and resources for parenting a child of a different race or culture; provide parents with an opportunity to enhance their knowledge, skills, capabilities, strengths, and limits, and to assess their ability to parent transracially and transculturally; and provide parents with resource material on subjects that relate to transracial/cultural families (i.e., health, books, support groups, camps). The following sections describe effective parent training programs.

An Insider's Guide to Transracial Adoptions

Pact: An Adoption Alliance has designed a manual, *An Insider's Guide to Transracial Adoptions* [Steinberg & Hall 1998a] as a resource book and training tool for foster and adoptive parents. (This manual also contains materials that apply to both domestic and international adoptions.) The manual helps parents develop a more in-depth understanding of how race impacts a child "being raised across racial lines," and provides a resource for parents facing the "predictable challenges of development for all members of transracial families."

The goals of the *Guide* are to describe the phases of building positive racial identity, compare the identity formation "of people of color with white people," and to identify issues that transracially adopted children will experience at various ages and developmental phases. The manual is divided into three general categories: racial identity, family life, and adoption issues.

- **Racial identity.** This section includes topics on developing identity (i.e., Asian, Black, Native American, Latino, biracial, and unknown racial identity), acknowledging differences, making connections (networking), and parenting tools.

- **Family matters.** This section includes such topics as parenting issues; birth family, extended family, and sibling issues; single parent, blended family, gay/lesbian, and international adoption family issues; and special needs issues (i.e., posttraumatic stress disorders, exposure to substance abuse).

- **Adoption.** This section describes the developmental stages (infancy, preschool, school-age, teen and young adult) and addresses issues the child might experience at each stage.

The trainer's guide has suggested agendas for one-, three-, five-, or ten-session workshops. (See Appendix C for an excerpt.)

Parenting Resource Manual

NACAC has developed the *Parenting Resource Manual* for adoptive parents who have adopted transracially (domestically or internationally) [Cunningham & Bower 1998]. The manual is also targeted for foster parents and prospective adoptive and foster parents contemplating raising a child of a different race or culture.

The manual is a compilation of numerous articles written by experts, parents, and youth who have experienced transracial or transcultural placements. The articles are divided into eight sections: background information, parenting skills, youth, medical/hair care, culture camps, cultural competence with agencies, racism, and resources.

- **Background.** Articles related to transracial placements and adoptions.

- **Parenting skills.** Articles that discuss parenting and approaches to developing positive identities (racial, cultural, and personal).

- **Youth.** Articles that reflect experiences of young adults from foster care and adoptive transracial or transcultural families.

- **Medical/hair care.** Articles that discuss the health and cosmetic needs of children of color.

- **Culture camps.** Features articles on culture camps.

- **Cultural competence.** Articles that address the need for cultural and competency within agencies.

- **Racism.** Articles that focus on the experiences of transracial families and strategies to confront and cope with racism.

- **Resource directory.** This includes a listing of organizations with which families can network, culture camps, books, book catalogues, videos and audiocassettes, and internet addresses throughout the country. Parent support groups throughout the United States and Canada are listed to help families network with their local community groups.

Training Videos

I have developed a series of three training videos for parents who have or are considering transracial/cultural adoptions. The video provides parents with information about the children's special needs, parenting tasks, and impact of transracial adoptions.

- **"The Impact of Transracial Adoption on the Adopted Child and The Adoptive Family."** This video identifies how transracial adoption affects the child's personal feelings about herself, her birth family and community of origin; the child's interaction with the adopted family and adopted community;

the nuclear and extended family's reaction to the adopted child; and how the family can manage the impact of a transracial adoption [Crumbley 1997a].

- **"Parenting Tasks, Goals and Challenges in Transracial Adoptions."** This video presents a psychosocial rationale on the parenting tasks with children adopted transracially, parental resources and capabilities, and information and networks parents must access and provide their adopted child and themselves [Crumbley 1997b].

- **"Special Needs of Minority Children Adopted Transracially."** This video discusses the child's need for cultural and positive racial identity, surrogate role models, cultural and community interaction, skills and explanations to cope with prejudice and discrimination, and specific skills that parents can use to address the minority child's needs [Crumbley 1997c].

The tapes can be used in groups or individually, with or without a trainer or facilitator. The handouts that accompany each tape are designed to be followed while viewing the tape; these handouts summarize the topics being discussed in outline form.

Leader's Guide for Preparation for Transracial/ Cross-cultural Fostering/Adopting

The Kentucky Department of Social Services' training curriculum and leader's guide were developed for prospective parents considering transracial foster care or adoption [Sturgeon 1996]. The purpose of the training is to prepare parents by educating them on the issues of parenting, identity, and the impact of transracial/transcultural placement on the family and child.

The training begins with a list of questions for the parents to answer to assess their initial strengths and limits regarding issues of parenting, attitudes towards race, and understanding of racial/cultural identity. The curriculum then identifies the tasks of parenting a child of a different racial/cultural background and differences between raising a child of the same background from a child whose background is different.

Training on identity focuses the participants' attention to the existence of prejudice and discrimination, the role of positive racial/cultural identity in counteracting the effects of prejudice and discriminations, and methods of developing positive identity and self-esteem. Participants are also made aware of the prejudice and discrimination they may experience from friends, neighbors, and family as a result of being a transracial family.

The training provides experiential exercises, didactic information, and used videos to help families determine their readiness for a transracial placement, prior to child being placed in their home. This final determination is based on the agency's evaluation and the family's self-assessment.

NACAC Training Curriculum

NACAC has developed a training curriculum for parents who may adopt or foster a child of another race, culture, or ethnicity [Bower 1998b]. The curriculum presents agencies or parent groups with issues related to transracial or transcultural adoption or foster care. The curriculum is designed as an educational tool for current or prospective parents—not as a screening tool to select or eliminate potential adoptive or foster families. (See Appendix D for an excerpt.)

The training curriculum is intended to assist parents in making informed decisions about their capability to parent a child of another race, culture, or ethnicity, and is divided into seven training modules. Each module provides objectives, agenda/timeline-training materials, and notes to the trainer.

- **Module 1: Motivation.** This section has parents evaluate their reasons for fostering or adopting transracially or transculturally. The anticipated outcome of this module is that parents consider information they are provided about the child's needs before fostering or adopting.

- **Module 2: Personal values.** The goal of this module is for parents to evaluate their personal activities toward people different from themselves before fostering or adopting. The end result is the parent's identification of personal prejudice, attitudes, and assumptions.

- **Module 3: Family.** This module equips parents with methods of protecting the adopted or foster child from damaging statements and interactions with extended family members.

- **Module 4: Home.** This module provides parents with methods of making their home more culturally integrated, comfortable, and compatible with the child's racial or cultural origin.

- **Module 5. Community.** This module introduces parents to important resources and the importance of networking with the child's community of origin, prior to and following placement.

- **Module 6: Cultural identity.** This module teaches parent techniques for developing the child's racial identity and incorporating the child's culture into the family's daily activities and routines.

- **Module 7: Racism.** This module helps parents understand the impact of prejudice and discrimination on the child (i.e., identity, esteem, opportunities, and rights), and equips them with skills to survive and confront discrimination, prejudice and racism.

- **Conclusion.** This section allows parents to assess their strengths and abilities and to identify any limits that need enhancing to parent transracially or transculturally.

Recommendations on Training Programs

Most of the materials require qualified trainers. The training programs appear to be flexible, collapsible, or expandable, depending on the training needs, number of participants, and time available for training. Trainer's guides should be used and requested to assist in the preparation of a curriculum, format, and materials.

I strongly recommend that the trainers have the opportunity to be participants themselves in any curriculum they are teaching. That experience will help them understand the feelings that participants may have, and will give them familiarity with other training approaches.

References

Bower, J. W. (1998a). *Self-awareness tool*. St. Paul, MN: North American Council on Adoptable Children.

Bower, J. W. (1998b). *Training curriculum*. St. Paul MN: North American Council on Adoptable Children.

Closs, G., Frazier, C., Hudson, B., Lee, L., Le Roi, M., & Valazquez, I. (1995). *Multiethnic parenting assessment guide*. Hartford, CT: Connecticut Department of Children and Family Services.

Crumbley, J. (1997a). *The impact of transracial adoption on the adopted child and the adoptive family* [video]. Philadelphia, PA: Action Duplication, Inc.

Crumbley, J. (1997b). *Parenting, tasks, goals and challenges in transracial adoptions* [video]. Philadelphia, PA: Action Duplication, Inc.

Crumbley, J. (1997c). The special needs of minority children adopted transracially [video]. Philadelphia, PA: Action Duplication, Inc.

Cunningham, S., & Bower, J. (1998). *Parenting resource manual*. St. Paul, MN: North American Council on Adoptable Children.

Hall, B., & Steinberg, G. (1998). *Below the surface*. San Francisco, CA: Pact Press.

Minnesota Department of Human Services. (1990). *Worker's assessment guide for families adopting cross-racially/cross-culturally*. St. Paul, MN: Author.

New York State Citizen's Coalition for Children, Inc. (1998*). Struggle for identity: Issues in transracial adoptions* [video]. Ithaca, NY: PhotoSynthesis Productions.

Steinberg, G., & Hall, B. (1998a). *An insider's guide to transracial adoption.* San Francisco, CA: PACT Press.

Steinberg, G., & Hall, B. (1998b). *Trainer's guide.* San Francisco, CA: PACT Press.

Sturgeon, V. (1996). *Leader's guide for preparation for transracial/cross-cultural fostering/adopting.* Lexington, KY: Kentucky Department for Social Services Division of Family Services.

Chapter Four
Preparing Children and Families for Placement

The stability of any placement depends on the interaction between the family and the child. The older the child, the more influence and impact she will have on the stability of the placement. The average age of the child waiting to be adopted is 8 years. The average time in foster placement prior to adoption is three years. The average age of children removed from their parents or caregivers and coming into the welfare system is 4 years [Maza 1998]. It is therefore essential to consider the child's past experiences as having a major impact on the stability and success of any foster placement or adoption.

Preparing the Child

You should begin to prepare and assess the child prior to the child's placement with the foster or adoptive family. The degree of preparation is contingent upon the immediacy of the placement, the child's age, and the child's availability.

Preplacement Evaluation

The purpose of evaluation at this time is to begin an assessment of the child's readiness for a transracial placement or adoption and to determine the child's feelings, attitudes, racial experiences, and opinions about living in a transracial or transcultural family prior to placement. Workers may focus on the following:

- the child's feelings about living with a family (either permanently or temporarily) of a different race or culture;

- the child's perceptions of the challenges and positives of living with parents or children of a different racial or cultural background;

- the child's knowledge of attitudes toward and experiences with people from other races and cultures;

- the child's perceptions about how he imagines being treated by the foster or adoptive parents, their children, extended family, and community;

- the child's perception of what might be different, what the child might miss, or how she might change when living with a different racial or cultural family (i.e., food, music, art, language);

- how the child would want parents of a different race or culture to threat him;

- how the child would treat parents of a different race;

- how the child's treatment or relationship with a parent of a different race or culture would be different from a same-race adoptive of foster parent;

- the child's thoughts about whether it is important for her and the prospective parents to learn and share with each other their feelings and information about each other's race, culture, and attitudes (i.e., fears, prejudices, personal encounters), and how they would share and learn together (i.e., activities, cultural events);

- what aspects of the child's culture, activities, and traditions he wants to continue in his new family (i.e., music, food, art) and how (i.e., display art, play music, include food in family meals, have friends over, go to neighborhood or community of racial/ cultural origin);

- the child's willingness to explore and participate in cultural activities of the prospective parents;

- what experiences the child has had with racial prejudice or discrimination in general, and with the race of her prospective parents specifically; and

- the child's thoughts about how these experiences have affected her feelings toward people from the group who mistreated her (i.e., Does she think that all members from that group will also be prejudiced or discriminate?).

The purposes of these questions are to assess the various factors that will come to bear in a transracial/transcultural placement:

- the importance of the child maintaining his racial and cultural identity,

- the child's personal values and attitudes toward other cultures and races,

- the child's knowledge of and willingness to participate in the prospective parent's culture, tradition, and heritage,

- the child's awareness of the impact of living in a transracial or transcultural family,

- the child's positive experiences or negative encounters with prejudice or discrimination from members of her prospective parents' racial/cultural group and how these experiences have impacted her perception of the prospective family and their community, and

- the level at which the child is ready to initiate contacts with the prospective parents of a different race or culture (i.e., day visits, weekends, immediate placement).

Case Study #4

This case study is an example of separate and joint assessments of prospective parents and siblings for a transracial adoption. The study highlights the siblings and foster parents' readiness for adoption, the ambivalence a child may experience, and the parents' need for preparation.

Evaluation and Recommendation for Adoption

Siblings: Sherri, age 8, biracial; Mary, age 6, white; and David, age 4, biracial

Prospective Parents: Mr. and Mrs. J (foster parents), white/ Amish

Dates of Evaluation: Children alone 6/15, Children and parents on 6/23, and parents alone on 6/23

Reason for the Referral

CYS (an adoption agency) has requested an evaluation be done with the three children, presently residing with the J family for three years as foster children. The request was prompted by the J family's request to adopt the children and Sherri's reluctance to be adopted because of feeling disliked "for being the only person with dark skin" in their Amish church, school, and community. Sherri revealed these feelings to her foster parents and caseworker.

Identifying and Background Information

Mr. and Mrs. J are a white couple who are active residents of their Amish community. Mr. and Mrs. J have been married for 13 years. After one and one-half years into their marriage, they realized there would be difficulty having children. They subsequently became foster parents to 16 children over approximately four years. The children have been white, Black, and biracial.

Mr. and Mrs. J, 38 and 31 years of age respectively, now have five foster children in residence, all of whom they intend to adopt. Two of the children (18 months and 11 years old) are white and unrelated. The 18-month (who they already adopted) has Rubinstein-Tayhi Syndrome, while the 11-month-old is classified as trainable mentally retarded. The other three children are siblings: Sherri, age 8, biracial (Black and white); Mary, age 6, White; and David, age 4, also biracial (Black and white).

Sherri lived with her birth parents for the first five years of her life. Her birth father was often in the home; however, mother had other boyfriends during their relationship. Both parents abused alcohol and engaged in physical and verbal abuse.

Sherri also witnessed physical and verbal fights between her older sister (now age 18) and her birth mother. Her sister was in placement from age 9 to 17. Sister's initial placement was due to having sexual and physical abuse. Sherri was sexually abused in her birth mother's home by a cousin and her birth father. She is able to give detailed information regarding the abuse. She has been in therapy since placement.

Sherri was frequently responsible for her siblings when living with her birth parents, in addition to caring for her birth mother when she was periodically incapacitated. Her siblings were placed with Mr. and Mrs. J shortly after their birth mother's incarceration for disorderly conduct.

Mary lived with her birth parents for the first three of her life. Her home situation was also marked by verbal, physical, and alcohol abuse by birth mother and boyfriend. Mary's father was white but not her birth mother's boyfriend. Further information about her father is not documented. There is no known history of physical or sexual abuse. Mary has been with her siblings in the J family since placement.

David lived with his birth mother for the first year of his life. His birth father is the same as Sherri's and was often in the home. The parents' interaction and behavior continued to be violent and abusive. There is no known history of physical or sexual abuse; however, due to the lack of custodial care, David was also placed with his siblings. His placement history and involvement with the J family is the same as his siblings.

Developmental History

All the children reportedly negotiated normal physical and developmental milestones appropriate to their respective ages. Each child's social and emotional development in the areas of impulse control, attention span, accepting limits, socialization skills and manners appear age appropriate.

Sherri has an outgoing and pleasant personality. She presents a positive, resilient, and cooperative attitude. There is a tendency to take on a parental role with her siblings, which may be a carry-over from the child care responsibilities she assumed while living with her birth mother.

Sherri attended a preschool while with her birth mother. During her first year in placement, it was decided that she might benefit more from parental attention rather than formal schooling. Sherri has recently completed the first grade with above average grades, and has been promoted to the second grade beginning September 1991.

Special developmental concerns will need continued attention throughout Sherri's emotional development because of the sexual abuse she experienced by her cousin and birth father at approximately 4 or 5 years old.

Mary has a friendly but somewhat quiet and shy demeanor. She is thoughtful and contemplative before speaking or responding to questions. Once trust is established, she is warm, open, and affectionate.

Developmentally, Mary appears to be on track. Her most recent intelligence tests categorized her in the average range of intellectual functioning. Mary had some difficulty adjusting to kindergarten, specifically letter identification and class participation. However, she did successfully complete the year and has been promoted to the first grade.

David is an alert, shy, and affectionate child. He is prone to "will" struggles and tantrums. His verbal, emotional, and physical development, however, appears to also be on target. No formal testing has been done, to date.

Children's Attachment and Readiness for Adoption

All of the children's problem-solving skills and ability to differentiate, separate, and appropriately attach to significant others are normal for each child's respective ages. Each child is appropriately attached and bonded with their foster parents.

The attachment is evidenced by the children's ability to verbalize and demonstrate

- their family's rituals and routines of interaction and exchange of affection;

- parental expectations, limits, privileges, and reward systems;

- expression of feelings and descriptions of routines that provide safety, security, and protection; and

- Mr. and Mrs. J meeting their perceptions of the ideal parents.

Neither David nor Mary had any reservation about living permanently with the J family. At my first meeting with Sherri, she expressed a desire to live with a family of similar color and race. This desire was based on her need to experience a group identity with "people who looked like (her)" and to not be ostracized or "teased for looking different because of (her) color."

The seriousness of this need was reinforced by her willingness to leave her siblings and Mr. and Mrs. J even though she admitted "loving them all." When asked if she would want to be adopted by the J family, if she was able to have interactions with people of her race, she responded by saying, "I'm not sure."

Sherri's response to this question changed to "yes" during my second interview with her. This change in response was due to

- her attendance at an interracial Amish-Mennonite church with her family, where she felt warmly accepted;

- interaction with biracial children while attending the church;

- enjoying the prospect of having "friends and maybe even a husband like her one day";

- the promise by her foster parents of attending the Amish-Mennonite's interracial school; and

- reassurance by the minister that racial teasing was "unacceptable and not tolerated."

Parents' Readiness to Adopt

Mr. and Mrs. J have approximately four years of experience as foster parents. They have been foster parents to 16 children who were white, Black, and biracial. Their child-rearing and limit-setting practices are based on alternative approaches to corporal punishment and expectation based on developmental milestones and theory (infancy, toddler, latency, and adolescence).

When asked how and/or if race is important in rearing a child, Mr. and Mrs. J answered yes. They further stated that a child's self-image, identity, and esteem are a result of positive and reassuring relationships and role models not only with parents, but with the child's racial and ethnic group as well.

When asked what, if any, preparation biracial children would need in their emotional developmental and socialization, Mr. and Mrs. J stated that preparation should involve

- developing a positive self-image and racial identity,

- preparation for prejudice and differential treatment on the basis of race and religion,

- a repertoire of responses to prejudice and discrimination,

- a support system to counteract the negative impact of discrimination, and

- exposure to positive family and racial role models to offset negative stereotypes.

Mr. and Mrs. J attributed their sensitivity to the specialized socialization of a minority child to their personal experience with discrimination on the basis of their religion (Amish).

Mr. and Mrs. J then identified steps they were already instituting to address the needs of their biracial children in general, and Sherri specifically. The steps included enrolling Sherri in an integrated Amish-Mennonite church, networking with Amish foster and adoptive families with biracial children, and acquiring permission from their church bishop to involve and expose their children to culturally and racially specific social and educational activities outside the Amish community.

Involving Children in the Placement Process

Involve the child in the pre- and postplacement processes. You should provide him with information about what is going on, what is about to happen, and other information, such as the following:

- how often and how long visits will be;

- where and what the child, parents, and family will do during the visits;

- what input or influence the child has in the decision to continue the preplacement contact or the decision to pursue placement;

- how the child will make her feelings about the placement known (i.e., confidential and to whom);

- what behaviors and feelings will let the child and others know if the placement should be discontinued or continued; and

- how long and what activities need to be tried to determine if the child should or shouldn't remain with the family (i.e., communication, quality time, play time, school, work, or cultural).

Supporting Children During Placement

You should help the child prepare for the emotional issues and impact of transracial adoption or placement with activities such as the following tasks:

- Help the child identify and verbalize the feelings and questions he has about adoption and foster care, in general, and about transracial families specifically. Help the child ask questions about why the family wants a child of a different race or culture, whether they previously had a child of a different race in their family, or whether the parents have friends or neighbors of the child's race.

- Identify sources, methods, and interactions with the prospective parent, family, and community that will help answer and address the child's questions and emotional feelings. Identify the structure of contacts, meetings, activities, conversations, and settings in which children can ask their questions and then see how the families live (i.e., home visits, agency meetings, dinner or lunch activities, movies).

- Prepare the child for the reactions people may have to transracial families. Prepare the child for stares, curious looks, or the lack of recognition when she is with a transracial family or she is the only person of her race/culture in the prospective foster/adoptive family's community.

- Provide the child with explanations and a repertoire of responses to peoples' reactions. Explain the reactions and how to respond by perhaps ignoring, by speaking out, or by getting help from her adoptive/foster parents.

- Help the child draw from her experiences of being treated differently as a method of building on her strengths and coping skills (i.e., experience of being a foster child). Have the child share experiences and memories of being mistreated or discriminated against and how she handled the situation.

- Increase the child's comfort level with different races and cultures and with being a minority by exposing him to other racial and cultural activities, groups, and communities. Take the child to activities in which he is in the minority (i.e., movies, stores, malls, and restaurants) to enhance his coping skills and tolerance of other peoples' reactions.

- Connect the child with other children living in transracial or transcultural families by phone, mail, groups, or videos to facilitate the child's questions.

- Arrange activities and meetings between the child and transracial families so that the child can "see what it's like" in the family and community (i.e., the prospective parents' and the child's, if possible).

- Identify methods of developing and maintaining the children's racial and cultural identities, as well as their family identity and origin. Identify educational, social, cultural, religious, or recreational activities and organizations that the children might contact. Discuss how and when they can stay in contact with their friends, family, and community.

- Identify the types of attitudes, behaviors, and values the child and the prospective parents will need to live together as a transracial family (i.e., respect, incorporate racial/cultural difference in family, allow racial/cultural connections).

- Help the child identify both the positive aspects of and challenges to living in an adoptive or foster family, in general, and a transracial family specifically. Discuss her needs or desire for permanency, safety, consistency, and nurturing. Also discuss issues of loss (i.e., family, culture) and differential treatment as a foster or adopted child. Discuss if the positives outweigh the negatives.

- Help the child develop a process that will assist her in determining her readiness to live in a transracial/cultural family. Discuss when, how, and with whom she can discuss her experiences with and opinion of the prospective family and her feelings about being adopted or placed transracially. The child should also know what impact her feelings or opinions will have on the decision of whether she will be placed with a transracial family.

Preparing the Family

You will see that the major differences between foster and adoptive parents involve the change in the roles and goals of foster parents who become adoptive parents and in the child's need to accept their foster parents' new role, goals, and relationship with them and the agency as adoptive parents. (These transitional issues are not experienced when the child has only had an adoption relationship with their parents.)

You will need to help foster parents understand how their role and goals may change

- from temporarily taking care of the child to being a permanent family,

- from helping the agency reunite the child with his birth parent/family to legally keeping and making the child a member of their family,

- from working for an agency and being paid for the child care to being totally and independently responsible for the child, and

- from being subordinate to the child's birth family to having more legal entitlements and authority than the birth family.

These changes in roles and goals result in many emotional issues and questions for the child and foster/adoptive parent, despite their mutual attachment, bonding, and length of residence together. Many of these transitional issues and questions will not be resolved prior to the adoption. Identifying and normalizing these issues and setting up a process for addressing these issues and questions with the child and foster/adoptive parents, however, are appropriate tasks when preparing families for adoption.

Myth #6: Knowing about a child's racial/cultural identity and needs is not necessary to consider when deciding to foster or adopt transracially/transculturally. Meeting a child's racial and cultural identity needs should not be a determining factor in deciding to adopt transracially/transculturally. In addition, being able to provide a child with a safe and permanent home should be the paramount consideration when prospective parents determine their ability to adopt or foster, whether same race or transracially/transculturally.

Response: Permanency of a placement or adoption is directly associated with the child's ability to attach and feel accepted. Attachment can be enhanced and strengthened if the child feels her racial/cultural and family of origin is also accepted.

Another predictor of permanency in placements is the parents' preparation and understanding of out-of-home care and adoption issues. Educating foster and adoptive families about the issues of race and family origin will allow families to feel informed. Feeling informed reduces the family's ambivalence. Consequently, the families are more committed to and definite about their decisions to foster or adopt a child.

It is imperative that we help foster parents and children realize that experiencing these transitional issues and questions are not necessarily a negative reflection or their attachment, bonding, and readiness to adopt and that these issues, questions, and experiences are inherent to adoptions in general and transracial or transcultural adoptions specifically.

Chapter Five

Identifying Parenting
Tasks and Skills

Transracial adoption and foster care will challenge you as practitioners to support parents as they help their children develop positive racial/ethnic identities and at the same time deal with prejudice and discrimination. These challenges require specific tasks, skills, and capabilities of the parents. This chapter outlines some of those capabilities and describes specific tasks. The chapter concludes with an explanation of prejudice, discrimination, and racism that parents can use.

As discussed in Chapter 2, there are many subtle (and not-so-subtle) ways that the impact of transracial placement may be manifested in children, family members, and in the community. Practitioners can support parents with the challenge by encouraging the **multidimensional bonding and attachments** that will need to occur on an emotional as well as a cultural level. The family will need to engage in bonding and attachment, just as same-race families do. This process will need to address racial, cultural, and family-of-origin issues and should include the following processes:

- Validating and acknowledging the child's losses and grief (racial and family);

- Anticipating testing by the child of the adoptive/foster family (i.e., loyalty, trust, motivation, fairness);

- Allowing the child to pursue, search, or maintain her racial and family identities;

- Planning how to integrate the child's racial, cultural, and family identities with the adoptive or foster family's;

- Acknowledging mutual fears, prejudices, and stereotypes—and working to change them; and

- Educating and interacting within each other's family, culture, and community.

These bonding and attachment processes also need to occur between the child and her foster or adopted siblings, friends, and the extended family of the adoptive or foster parents. I myself heard one birth child say to a parent, "You may treat them like they're your children, but they're just foster kids to me, not my brothers or sisters." An adoptive parent recalled her birth child saying, "You and dad may become this kid's parents, but this isn't a package deal. I'm not his brother."

Foster and adoptive parents have reported limiting or ending contacts with friends and relatives who were unable to accept their child's racial difference. This is a practice that has carried over from parents in same-race adoptions or placement when people have had difficulty accepting the child's difference in family origin.

> **Myth #7:** Children in transracial homes should be raised as if they are the same race and culture of the adoptive or foster family. The child should adapt to the family, not the family to the child. Shared racial identity and culture are necessary for family attachment and bonding.

Response: When a family adopts or fosters transracially, they not only become a blended family (as in same-race placements), but also an interracial family. Although the family may perceive and raise the child racially or culturally the same as themselves, society still perceives and assigns the child a racial identity and status. Therefore, the child will need help in developing her own positive racial/cultural identity, especially if she might encounter prejudice and discrimination on the basis of nationality, race, culture, or language.

Although the adoptive or foster family may continue to perceive themselves as members of the dominant culture, society may perceive them as an integrated or interracial family. The adoptive or foster family may also need to be prepared for prejudice and discrimination from perhaps their own race as well as the child's.

The National Adoption Information Clearinghouse (NAIC) has identified several issues that prospective parents should consider when preparing for or contemplating transracial placements:

- They should evaluate their personal values, beliefs, and attitudes about race.

- They should consider their lifestyle and the changes that may be necessary (i.e., geographically relocating, social life).

- They should consider adopting siblings [NAIC 1997].

In addition, Lin identified several "do's and don'ts" for parents to help a child develop positive racial and ethical identity after encountering prejudice, racism, or discrimination:

- Try to emphasize your commitment to the child despite the child's rejection or confusion when encountering racism or prejudice.

- Acknowledge the child's pain related to prejudice and discrimination.

- Validate and accept the child's anger when she is in pain.

- Provide examples of confronting and coping with experiences of prejudice and discrimination.

- Don't make excuses for racism, prejudice, or discrimination.

- Don't feel guilty for your race's prejudice and discrimination.

- Don't expect to have all the answers for your child. Say "I don't know" and get help or advice. You don't have your child's racial background or experiences [Lin 1998].

How do parents address these issues? Practitioners must ensure that they have certain skills and capabilities, which are described in the following section.

Parental Skills and Capabilities

The Minnesota Department of Health and Human Services' *Worker Assessment Guide for Families Adopting Transracially and Cross-Culturally* [1990] identifies several capabilities that are desirable in parents who wish to adopt crossculturally or transracially:

- They have a sense of their own values and attitude about the racial and cultural differences of others and of how their attitudes and values were formed.

- They have an understanding of why and how racism, prejudice, and discrimination exist and operate and how to counteract their existence and effects.

- They have the ability to attach and empathize with a child of a different racial, socioeconomic, and cultural origin.

- They have the capacity to provide the child with positive racial and cultural experiences and information.

- They have the ability to prepare the child for reentry and reconnection with her racial and cultural community.

- They reside in a community that provides the child with same-race adults, peer relationships, and role models.

- They have the capacity to incorporate and participate in crosscultural and racial activities.

- They acknowledge that the family becomes an interracial family following the child's membership.

- They have the capacity, skills, and tolerance needed to appropriately manage people's responses (i.e., prejudice and discrimination) to them as an interracial and transracial adoptive family.

- They have the willingness and capacity to develop the skills and implement the tasks necessary in developing a child's positive cultural and racial identity.

- They have the interests, skills, and resources to meet the child's dietary, skin, hair, and health needs.

- They appreciate the child's differences in racial, cultural, and family origin, while simultaneously meeting the need for "full membership" in the family.

Parenting Tasks

This section discusses seven tasks for parents who foster or adopt transracially/transculturally. You must assist parents in preparing for and accomplishing these tasks to meet the special needs of children in foster or adoptive transracial families.

Before you go through those specific tasks, though, here are some general recommendations for your work with parents. Edna Bautista provides suggestions in parenting a biracial or multiethnic child, based on interviews and recommendations from five adult adoptees:

- Tell the multiethnic child that she is just as normal as other people;

- Tell the child not to be ashamed of expressing his differences and feelings;

- Emphasize the child's similarities to and differences from others;

- Involve and connect the child to other multiethnic or biracial children;

- Help and allow the child to explore, search, and select her racial and cultural identity;

- Help the child to feel proud of his racial or cultural origins; and

- Prepare the child for what racial identity society may assign her and for the treatment associated with that assigned identity [Bautista 1998].

Holt International Children's Services has also developed a series of questions that parents should address if they are considering intercountry adoption or parenting a child from another country:

- What are your opinions about race and the characteristics that you associate with different racial groups (i.e., Asian, Indian, Latino)?

- How do you feel about public stares and unwelcome attention?

- Will you raise your child to have your own racial/cultural identity?

- How will you raise your child to develop her own racial/cultural identity?

- How will you educate and sensitize yourself to what it's like to be nonwhite and grow up in a white society?

- How will you feel when people see you with your child and assume that you are in an interracial marriage?

- What are your motivations for adopting (rescuing, wanting to feel appreciated) [Holt 1995]?

- Do you feel that it is necessary to learn about the child's culture?

Task #1: Acknowledge the Existence of Prejudice, Racism, and Discrimination

This task requires the parents to recognize that racism, prejudice, and discrimination exist. This admission will help parents avoid inadvertently denying and minimizing the child's experiences or excusing racist, prejudicial, or discriminating behavior.

Parents also need to tell *and* show the child that other minority groups can be successful and make positive achievements if given equal opportunities and resources; that members from other racial or minority groups deserve equal rights; that racism, prejudice, and discrimination are incorrect; and that other racial groups are equal to members from the dominant group.

Task #2: Explain Why the Child's Racial or Cultural Group Is Mistreated

This task requires parents to explain and define racism, prejudice, discrimination, and bigotry. Parents can enhance the child's coping skills by helping him understand behaviors as not being either good or bad. By understanding the functions and reasons for the behaviors, the child can also increase his range of responses beyond anger or retaliation.

Task #3: Provide the Child with a Repertoire of Responses to Racial Discrimination

This task minimizes the child's feelings of helplessness. The child's identity can be more positive if she perceives herself and her racial group as empowered with choices, resources, and the ability to acquire and protect their rights. This repertoire of responses may include

- selective confrontation or avoidance;

- styles of confrontations (passive, aggressive);

- individual, legal, institutional, or community resources and responses (i.e., grievances, suites, NAACP, protests);

- priorities and timing (when and when not to avoid issues);

- goal-oriented responses rather than unplanned emotional reaction; and

- institutional/organizational strategies, such as positioning, coalitions, and compromise.

> **Myth #8**: Love is enough. The only thing a transracially adopted or foster child needs is a loving and caring family. Consequently, any emotional issues resulting from being in out-of-home care will be remedied, or may not even occur. In fact, the younger they're adopted or placed (i.e., infancy) the less likely children are to experience these emotional issues (i.e., loss, grief, rejection, etc.).

> **Response:** The child's attachment or bond to his foster/ adoptive parent will not stop him from asking why his birth parents (family, country) didn't keep him, accusing or questioning the foster/adoptive parents' motives for taking him away from his family or country, or from feeling the loss of leaving his family or country, fantasizing about being with his family, race, or country. An attachment with the foster/adoptive parents may not compensate for the child's developmental issues (i.e., self-esteem, personal/racial identity). Adoptive/foster parents may not be the child's reference, source of identity, or role models for answering such questions as, "What am I going to be like when I grow up?" or "Am I going to be like my 'real' mom or dad?"

Case Study #5

This case study involves one minority family's confrontation with the prejudices and discriminations of the dominant group. (The events in this case took place in the early 1960s and predate the Civil Rights Act.)

An African American family took annual trips to visit relatives who lived in the South. Shortly after driving into their relative's town, the 11-year-old boy in the family noticed that a white police office was directing his father to pull their car over. The police officer got out of his car, walked over to the child's father, called him "boy," and instructed him to get out of the car. The child heard the police officer give his father further instructions: don't look a white man in the eye, get off the sidewalk if a white person is walking by, use facilities and entrances for Blacks only, avoid facilities that said "for whites only," and don't be on the streets after a certain time. The child recalled that his father responding with "Yes, sir" throughout the police officer's instructions. The young child became angry while listening to this conversation—mostly with his father for letting the officer talk to him that way.

After the officer drove away, the father noticed his son's anger and responded with the following: "My goal was to get you, your brother, sisters, and your mom safely through town and to our relatives. I didn't want any of our relatives to get into trouble after we leave because of what I did or said. I've got that police officer's name and badge number, and I'll be back and other people (African Americans) like us will be back to march and change things."

The young child was then able to see his father's strength in a different way. The child hadn't seen his father's actions as based in strength, but he also remembered not being strong enough himself to have accepted the treatment his father had received. Now a man, the child realized in retrospect that his father's style of confrontation, at that moment, was passive and that his approach was compromise and avoidance. The child also realized that was not the time to be assertive or aggressive and that his father's priority was the family's safety. (The father's later reaction would be part of a collective coalition—the civil rights movement.) The father's behavior indicated that his response to the police officer was dictated by goals, not emotions or anger.

Task #4: Provide the Child with Role Models and Positive Contact Within the Community

The need for this task is based on two assumptions: that children from racial or cultural groups who experience prejudice and discrimination will need positive support and reinforcements from their family, role models, and their community to counteract negative racial identity and feelings of inferiority, and that same-race role models and the child's exposure to her culture and community are essential in counteracting negative stereotypes about their racial group.

Parents of a different race from their child are quite capable of modeling and helping the child develop various identities (i.e., gender, class). Counteracting the racial identity projected by a racially conscious or discriminating society, however, requires positive exposure to same-race role models or experiences. These contacts and experiences require interacting with the child's racial or cultural community, providing the child with information about his history and culture, and providing an environment that includes the child's culture on a regular basis (i.e., art, music, food, religion, school, living in an integrated community).

This task requires that the parent be comfortable with being a minority when interacting in the child's community and with sharing the role of modeling with members from the child's race. Same-race contacts and experiences function to counteract negative stereotypes, teach the child how to implement the repertoire of response, and provide a respite from being a minority (i.e., the only child of color, the object of stares, or needing to prove ones equality).

Task #5: Prepare the Child for Discrimination

Providing the child with information on what others may think about her racial identity helps her develop better coping skills and methods of maintaining a positive identity. The feeling of self-confidence in her ability to cope and appropriately respond, reinforces a positive self-image and identity. Using same-race role models may be a helpful resource for information and preparation if the adoptive parent has not experienced discrimination similar to the child's racial or cultural group (i.e., double standards, slander, interracial dating, and gender issues).

Case Study #6

This case study provides an example of how to prepare a child for prejudice and discrimination and describes the meeting of a support group of parents who have adopted transracially. The case study depicts an adoptive white couple who are concerned about their adopted adolescent African American son wanting their permission to date the Caucasian daughter of one of their neighbors.

The adoptive parents asked the group for input and assistance in deciding whether or not they should give their adopted son permission, whether they should prepare him for how the young lady's parents might respond, and whether they should prepare him for how people might respond seeing an African American male teenager dating a white teenage girl.

The group responded with an unanimous "yes!"—The parents *should* give their son permission to date interracially. The group felt that to not give him permission was saying he was "not good enough to date or socialize with their white neighbors." The group also suggested that the parents

- prepare their son for either positive and negative responses from their neighbors;

- provide their son with explanations for why some neighbors might accept him as a friend of their daughter's, but not dating their daughter because of his race;

- describe to their son how the public might negatively react to interracial dating (i.e., comments, stares);

- provide their son with a variety of responses to public situation (i.e., when and how to anticipate, confront, or avoid situations);

- how to respond to the neighbors' positive or negative reaction; and

- how and when to request their (his parents') help or involvement if he experiences prejudice or discrimination.

Task #6: Teach the Child the Difference Between Responsibility to and for the Racial Cultural Group

This task relieves the child of feeling embarrassed or needing to apologize for his racial identity or group and of having to overcompensate or prove his worth because of his racial identity or negative stereotypes. As a result, the child is able to develop a commitment to both his cultural and racial group's accomplishments, resources, and empowerment.

The Clark Doll Test suggests that children are aware of differences in race as early as 4 years. The study also found that African American children became aware of the stigma associated with race as early as 6 years [Clark & Clark 1958]. (In this study, African American children selected white dolls as being preferable to black dolls.) Although parents cannot stop a child's exposure to racial prejudice, discrimination, and stereotypes, parents (adoptive, birth, same or different race) can help develop the child's positive racial identity necessary to counteract the effects of racial inferiority.

Task #7: Advocate on Behalf of Your Child's Rights and Entitlements

The purpose of this task is to provide the child with an environment that is conducive to the formation of a positive identity. The parent should advocate for social and educational experiences that are respectful, reflective, and sensitive to cultural diversity. Therefore, the parent may need to be prepared to correct or confront individual or institutional racism, prejudice, or discrimination, on behalf of their child and family.

As an advocate, the parent models for the child how to advocate for himself. The child also sees and feels his parents' protection, loyalty, and commitment, which are essential elements in attachment and bonding. Failing to confront prejudice and discrimination on the child's behalf is no longer optional once a parent adopts or fosters transracially.

Explaining Prejudice, Discrimination, and Racism

I would like to give an example of how children can pick up explanations and definitions of racism, prejudice, and discrimination from their environment and demonstrate how children in intercountry transracial adoptions can also experience prejudice, discrimination, racism, inferiority, and the emotional impact of being transracially adopted. This example describes a group session I held with Korean children internationally and transracially adopted.

I was invited by a group of parents who had transracially adopted children from Korea who asked me to address the following questions:

- Are our adopted children experiencing the impact of transracial adoption in a manner similar to children adopted domestically?

- Are our children experiencing differential treatment on the basis of their race?

- Is there a need to address our children's racial identity or should they be raised as "Americans"?

- Will we need to engage in parenting tasks similar to those parents who transracially adopted their children in this country?

After answering these questions from a hypothetical and theoretical prospective, I met with some of their children to accurately answer these questions. I met alone with 12 of their children, ranging in age from 5 to 12 years old. They had all been adopted by their parents between the ages of 11 years and 20 months. Some of the children knew each other. Prior to the meeting, the children were told they were going to talk with someone about adoption. After introductions, I asked the children if they knew what prejudice, discrimination, or racism meant. They were all unsure, but agreed "it was not a nice way to treat people." I then gave the following definitions to the children:

- Prejudice is being treated by people based on what they heard about you before meeting you.

- Discrimination is being treated differently because you are a different race or color.

- Racism is what causes people to tease you, or to say or do things to you because they think their race is better than yours.

Next, I asked the children if they had ever experienced prejudice, discrimination, or racism. All 12 of the children began waving their hands, anxiously wanting to tell their stories and share their experiences:

- being called a "Jap," "Chenk," having "yellow fever";

- being asked, "Where are your glasses?"; and

- being told, "You can't play sports because you're only good in math like all Chinese."

The youngest child in the group (age 5) was the last child to share her experience. When the group and I asked what was said to her, she responded, "Nothing." We asked her, "What were you not allowed to do?" Again her response was, "Nothing."

Then someone asked if she was treated differently. She responded "Yes." The group and I then asked, "Well, what happened?" She put a finger at the outside corner of each eye and pulled back the corners. The group responded in a roar, saying, "That's called slanty eyes." The 5-year-old said she wanted to have an eye operation "to make my eyes round." I responded by saying that there wasn't such a procedure. The children in the group assured me there was. I later found out they were correct.

The children then asked, "Why do people treat us this way?" I responded by asking them a series of questions.

- "Has anyone ever teased or said things about other kids you knew were wrong, but did it anyway because everybody else did?" All 12 arms flew up accompanied by embarrassed giggling and an enthusiastic, "Yeah!"

- "Have you teased, mistreated, or said things to other kids you knew were wrong, but did it because you were afraid you might get teased or mistreated for not going along with the crowd?" All 12 waved their arms and answered, "Yeah!"

- "Did you ever say bad things about a person before you got to know them, because you were afraid of them?" The unanimous response was again, "Yeah!"

- "Did you ever feel put down or bad and then put someone else down so that you'll feel better?"

- "Did you ever need to feel better than someone else to feel better about yourself?"

- "Did you ever make up stories about someone so that it would be OK to take or keep something someone else deserved?"

To all these questions, the children either raised their hands or giggled while their hands partially covering their faces in embarrassment. We then discussed how anyone (included them) could discriminate or be prejudiced (which they admitted with more embarrassing giggles and laughter) and that they would also be acting prejudiced if they disliked everyone from the same race of the kids who mistreated them.

The meeting ended with the children verbalizing and ventilating feelings bout being adopted and taken out of their country:

- "Why didn't my county and parents keep me?"

- "What was wrong with me or them?"

- "Sometimes I get tired of being the only one (Korean)."

- "I know I'm better off here (USA)."

- "I can't go back because I can't speak the language, but I'd like to see my country one day."

After the parents received this feedback, they were better able to understand the following issues:

- Their children were experiencing differential treatment on the basis of their race.

- Their children needed a positive racial and cultural identity to counteract the stereotypes and effects of differential treatment.

- Their children were feeling the impact of transracial adoption similar to children adopted in-country.

- They needed to implement parenting tasks specific to transracial adoptions.

- Children can understand prejudice, discrimination, and racism, if defined experientially at their age level.

Explanation and definitions of prejudice, discrimination, and racism are longitudinal and developmental. The complexity of definitions and explanations increase over time as children grow and mature. You should also emphasize to parents that definitions and explanations also need to be repeated over time. Listed below are various indicators that can help a parent decide when to begin addressing issues of race and identity:

- the child begins asking questions or making comments about identity (racial or family),

- the child begins to notice the racial difference between her and her adoptive or foster family,

- the child begins to share positive or negative race-related experiences outside the home, or

- the child needs to be prepared for racial encounters (i.e., prejudice, discrimination, employment, housing, dating, law enforcement, education).

Conclusion

Indications of a child's need for attention to her racial and cultural issues reoccur throughout her life. Parents may need to explain and define prejudice and discrimination again and again. The complexity of the explanations will increase as the child grows older and her questions increase in maturity. Foster/adoptive parents will constantly have to refer and reframe for the child the following explanations for racism, prejudice, and discrimination:

- the need to rationalize one's behavior,

- following the crowd,

- fear of retribution for not going along with the crowd,

- fear of the unknown,

- repeating and believing learned behaviors and traditions,

- the need to feel superior to others because of low self-esteem,

- fear of competition and loss of power,

- the need to maintain the status quo and hierarchy of power, and

- fear of racial extinction through interracial relationships.

References

Bautista, E. (1993). Mixed identity: How multiethnic children cope with their identity. *Child of Colors, 6*, 33-37.

Clark, K. B., & Clark, M. P. (1958). Racial identification and preference in Negro children. In E. E. Macoby, T. M. Newcombe, & E. Hartley (Eds.), *Education and psychological measurements* (pp. 89-97). New York, NY: Rinehart and Winston.

Holt International Children's Services. (1995). *Issues to consider before pursuing intercounty adoption.* Eugene, OR: Author.

Lin, J. L. (1998). Helping your child develop racial ethnic identity. In B. Cunningham & J. Bower (Eds), *Parenting resource manual* (pp. 191-194). St. Paul, MN: North American Council on Adoptable Children.

Minnesota Department of Human Services. (1990). Worker's assessment guide for families Adopting cross-racially/cross-culturally. St. Paul, MN: Author.

National Adoption Information Clearinghouse. (1997). Transracial and transcultural adoption. Washington, DC: Author.

O'Connor, R. (1998). Transracially adopted children's bill of rights. In G. Steinberg & B. Hall (Eds.), *An insider's guide to transracial adoption.* San Francisco, CA: Pact Press, 1998.

Chapter Six
Case Management

Your responsibilities have always included certain case management tasks, such as obtaining information about the child's educational history and performance levels, assisting parents in acquiring medical coverage for the child, acquiring financial subsidies and entitlements, and providing parents with the legal authority to which they are entitled. As you work with transracial families, you will need to carry out some management activities that are specific to the needs of transracial families, especially those needs related to education, health care and hygiene, community networking, parent education and support, and postplacement services. This chapter discusses those activities.

Educational Needs

Of course your primary responsibility is to facilitate the older child's adjustment and transition into a new educational environment (or to develop long-range plans for infants and younger children). For the transracial family, your case management responsibilities may also include the following:

- Evaluating an educational facility's ability to address the child's educational, racial, and cultural issues (i.e., diversity of staff, curriculum, student population, celebrated holidays, religions, races, gender and ethnic groups, and bilingual education).

- Helping the parents bring about necessary changes in the educational systems so that their child's emotional and cultural needs are addressed (i.e., contact persons in the school's administration).

- Educating child care and educational facilities about their need for cultural diversity and competence and the needs of children in transracial/cultural families.

- Planning with the family for the child or family's relocation to a different school or community, if the child's educational, racial, or cultural needs are not met.

Health Care and Hygiene Issues

There are inherent differences specific to racial and cultural groups, which are frequently the result of such physical differences as hair texture, skin tone, and pigmentation. Acquired differences are frequently a result of cultural traditions, practices, and lifestyles that may also be influenced by the environment as well. You may need to educate adoptive and foster parents about how these differences impact the child's health care and hygiene. Environmental, cultural, and physical differences may also impact the quality and status of the child's nutritional health, if he comes from certain countries or communities. Listed below are some case management responsibilities.

- Assisting the parents in obtaining medical examinations and treatment for the child that are sensitive to the child's race, culture, and nationality. For example, the child may have certain dental problems resulting to the absence of good dental practices.

- Facilitating the parents' education about hair care maintenance and hairstyles specific to the child's race, nationality, and culture, and connecting the parents and the child with resources that provide care, maintenance, and styling services (i.e., salons, barbers, cutteries, or hairstylists that are culturally diverse or located in the child's racial or cultural community).

- Facilitating the parents' education about skin care, sensitivities, and disorders that are specific to their child. Parents may need training in the types of cosmetics that compliment their child's skin tones. Some racial and/or cultural groups may require replacing skin oils with certain ointments. Children from other countries may be sensitive to certain clothing, materials, and chemicals to which they were not previously exposed.

- Facilitating the parents' education about the preferable meats, foods, fruits, vegetables, and seasonings that are specific to the child's racial and cultural origin. Children may have intestinal or allergic reactions to foods or seasonings that are not eaten in their country.

Community Networking

An important part of your role as case manager is to support parents as they provide their child with an opportunity to have same-race relationships, mentors, peers, positive cultural experiences, and education—all of which will enhance a positive racial/cultural identity development. Some of your responsibilities will include the following activities:

- Assisting the families in identifying and participating in communities, activities, and organizations of the child's racial/cultural origin;

- Encouraging the parents to provide their child with access to same-race mentors and peers who are personal friends of and socially interact with the family (i.e., family dinners, social activities);

- Connecting the parents to activities and experiences for the child that are culturally enriching and educational (i.e., culture camps, clubs, heritage retreats); and

- Planning with families to consider relocating to communities to ensure their own and their child's access to same-race relationships, mentors, and peers.

Parent Education and Support

It is your ongoing responsibility to help foster or adoptive parents develop the skills, cultural competence, and sensitivity they will need to raise a child of a different race, culture, or nationality. Activities for the case manager include the following:

- Assisting the family in diversifying and integrating their home and lifestyles (i.e., food, art, music, holidays, dress, furnishings, language) with customs and lifestyles of the child;

- Directing the family to organizations, agencies, conferences, and workshops that provide training for parents who are adopting or fostering transracially or transculturally;

- Referring families to parent support groups and adoptive and foster parent organizations that provide networks, information, and support to transracial/transcultural families;

- Connecting families to same-race agencies, organizations, and community groups that are willing to mentor, network, educate, and support transracial or transcultural families;

- Identifying for families resource materials that would be useful (i.e., book catalogs, publications, videos, internet exchanges, and websites); and

- Coordinating therapeutic referrals of families and children needing individual, group, or family therapy to address adoption, foster care, or transracial/transcultural issues.

Postplacement Services

You will be called on to provide a continuum of postplacement services that can be categorized as short-term, crisis, or intermittent. With transracial families, you may also need to offer services during specific developmental or transitional phases that the foster or adopted child, parents, and family experience.

The child may need assistance in addressing his feelings of inadequate racial or cultural identity or in searching for his identity. Parents may need support in coping with the personal or cultural rejection or accusations from their foster/adopted child experiencing losses or pursuing his identity. Parents may need suggestions in how and where they can network with agencies and organizations that can provide support and same-race experiences for their child through various developmental stages.

The child may be experiencing developmental or transitional issues related to loss, identity, or trust issues. The parents may be experiencing issues of disillusionment with foster care or the adoption due to unfulfilled expectations (i.e., end of the honeymoon phase). The extended family or birth siblings may feel betrayed by the parents' loyalty to the foster or adopted child, or the legal inclusion or entitlements of the foster or adopted child in legal wills or to property.

All of these services should be available following placement (foster or preadoption placement) and postadoption. Families should also be informed and reminded of these services. The short-term services are "as needed" and could be based on a "brief service model" of two to three months. The crisis services should be available upon "immediate need" lasting as long as necessary, or appropriately referred. Intermittent services should be arranged on a routine schedule, comparable to yearly medical examinations. Developmental or transitional services should be done or arranged during intermittent assessments for services, or anticipated phases and transitions of the child and family (i.e., age of child, or length or adoption or placement).

Part III

Professional Concerns

Chapter Seven
Staff Attitudes and Values

Adequately serving and supporting transracial foster and adoptive families demands that professional staff be well-prepared. Agencies and organizations must develop a value base, standards, and guidelines for practice and parenting in transracial adoption and foster care. Professionals need to conduct a self-assessment and clarification of their own personal values and attitudes about transracial parenting and the impact of these values and attitudes on their practice and families.

In addition, agencies and professionals need to provide training and education to staff about transracial adoptions and foster care to impact staff's attitudes, values, and quality of practice. Staff will need cultural sensitivity and competence to engage and interface with multicultural, transracial families, as well as children and communities of other races, ethnicities, and countries.

Values, Standards, and Guidelines
Agencies, organizations, and professionals must expand their dialogue beyond the question, "Is transracial adoptions and foster care right or wrong?" The reality is that transracial adoptions

and foster care are occurring. Professionals and organizations must now focus on assessing, selecting, training, and supporting families to adequately parent and meet the special needs of these children.

Therefore, agencies must develop standards, criteria, and guidelines based on research and information about the needs of children and parents in transracial adoptive and foster families. The results will be needs-based assessment tools, screening/recruitment and selection processes, and training/preparation programs. (See "Special Needs of Transracial Families," on p. 7.)

Adoption and foster care professionals and agencies do not need to recreate the wheel. Standards and guidelines for sound practice and parenting in same-race adoptions and foster care already exist. The field needs to test the validity and reliability of these standards and guidelines, however, by applying them to transracial/transcultural adoptions and foster care. (See "Parental Skills and Capabilities," on p. 66.)

Professionals must also evaluate and assess their values toward transracial adoptions and foster care. The child welfare profession and professionals are obviously not "value free." Debates of "good or bad" and positions of "pro or con" transracial adoptions and placement are indicative of values and attitudes.

The professionals' values can be communicated when they tell prospective parents that they can or they can not parent transracially, or when they state that special parenting is necessary or not necessary in transracial families. The types and quality of assessments, recruitment, selection, training, and preparation also reflect the professional's values and attitude, despite the agency or organization's position, policies, and procedures.

Cultural Sensitivity

Agencies and organizations will need to be culturally sensitive and competent to engage multicultural and transracial families, communities, and foster or adoptive children from other races, cultures, and countries, so that they can effectively teach parents to become culturally sensitive and competent in responding to the cultural and racial needs of their children. Cultural competency and sensitivity need to be developed on a staff and organizational level so that the staff and organization mutually reinforcing each other's policies and practices of cultural sensitivity and competency, and so that the staff and organization will be sensitive and competent enough to engage and interface with people on a "micro" level (individual client and families), as well as on a "macro" level (communities/neighborhoods/ intercountry).

Listed below are some effective activities that agencies can use in assisting staff develop racial/cultural sensitivity and competency.

• Provide staff with information about the culture, traditions, and values of the community and clients they serve.

• Develop approaches and techniques of intervening, joining, and engaging families and communities that respects their values, norms, and traditions.

• Standardize the respect and sensitivity to culture by including questions about culture in the collection of data, in assessment tools, treatment plans, and progress reports. The agency might also ask the client to evaluate the staff and the organization's cultural sensitivity and competence.

Preparing the Organization

A commitment to cultural competency and sensitivity needs to begin at organizational, decisionmaking, and administrative levels. The infrastructure, policies, and practices of cultural competency and sensitivity will then have organizational authorization and support. The following are organizational tasks that support and legitimize competent and culturally sensitive practices.

- Incorporate the concept of cultural competency and sensitivity as a mission, goal, objective, or strategy. Writing the organization's commitment, goals, and strategies into existing mission statements is one way to give organizational support at a decisionmaking level. Policy statements that identify practices, training, structures, committees, and staffing are another method of exemplifying the organization's commitment.

- Develop culturally/racially diverse advisory committees and keep staff involved on the planning, decisionmaking, managing, and operational levels. Identifying the authority to make changes in the organization's policies and practices and delegating that authority to these committees reinforces the staff and organization's verbal commitment.

- Standardize organizational sensitivity and competency policies, practices, and procedures through employment qualifications/ descriptions, routine training, quality assurance reviews, staff and organizational performance evaluations, and a standing culturally sensitive and competency committee to oversee the organization and staff's activities and compliance. Employment qualifications should include training, cultural competency, and sensitivity. Ongoing staff training should identify specific topics and required hours of training. Staff organizational and program evaluations should assess the policies, degree, and practices of cultural sensitivity and competency.

Chapter Eight
Recruitment

The Multiethnic Placement Act of 1994 (MEPA) required states to develop and implement plans for recruiting minority foster and adoptive families [DHHS 1995]. This chapter is intended to help you understand the barriers to recruitment and retention and to identify strategies for minimizing those barriers. In addition, it describes the components of effective recruitment programs. Finally, the chapter provides recommendations on how to identify, elicit, and connect with prospective foster and adoptive parents and how to retain parents through the preparation, pre-, and postselection processes.

Barriers to Recruitment

Those of us involved with adoption and foster care would like to be able to recruit and retain a racially diversified pool of foster and adoptive families, but we encounter many barriers. MEPA [1995] identified several problem areas and issues that states need to address in their recruitment plans:

- The lack of descriptive characteristics of children needing foster and adoptive families (i.e., racial/cultural percentages and community locations);

- Limited plans and strategies for targeting a racially and culturally diversified community;

- The need for methods of disseminating general and child-specific information to specific racial and cultural communities;

- The need for culturally competent staff to interact with racially, economically, and culturally diverse communities;

- Limited methods of overcoming linguistic differences between agencies and communities;

- The inaccessibility of family to recruitment, education, and preparation activities;

- Expensive fee structures and standards of age, education, family configurations, size, or proprietary status that might exclude or alienate racial, cultural, or socioeconomic groups of potential families;

- The inadequate use of interagency and interstate networks for identifying available racially and culturally diverse foster and adoptive families; and

- The need for procedures that expedite timely home studies, investigations, approvals, and certifications of prospective foster and adoptive families.

Myth #9: Blacks do not adopt.

Response: Black adoption has, historically, been a matter of what Hill calls "informal" adoption, where a child is taken into a home and reared as one's own child, but that relationship is never legalized in the courts. Because this practice had no legal sanction, and thus was never entered as an adoption statistic, the myth arose in this society that Blacks do not adopt. The fact is that, although Blacks adopted in large numbers, the practice of legal adoption is still a relatively new phenomenon for many Blacks, especially the working class [Hill 1972].

To further dispel the myth that Blacks do not adopt, Hill conducted a study for the National Urban League that had profound findings. He reported that each year Black families demonstrate their ability to "adopt" children with a placement rate more than ten times that of formal adoption agencies. Hill also found that for the year 1968, for all the Black children adopted, some 90% were adopted by the formal method (the comparable number for whites was 7%) [Ladner 1977].

Other studies indicate that when family composition, income, and age are the same, Blacks adopt at a rate 4.5 times greater than the white or Hispanic community [Gershenson 1984].

Myth #10: African American communities, professionals, and organizations (such as NABSW) are unapproachable and uncompromising regarding transracial adoptions and foster care and would rather have a child languish in foster care than be adopted.

Response: The African American community, families, and professionals can be effective educators, resources, and mentors to families who adopt or foster transracially and can be used as prospective families for children from other races or cultures (i.e., Caucasian or biracial). NABSW's [1994] statement is that:

NABSW is in full support of permanency planning for all children. We believe that too many children are placed in foster care unnecessarily and that often they remain in foster care too long. NABSW asserts the conviction that children should not be placed in foster homes or institutions when family preservation and family support services are more appropriately in the best interest of the child. When all reasonable efforts have been made to keep the child and family together, and when family preservation, family reunification, and relative placement have failed, then, and only then, should we seek adoption. Adoption should be within the same race. Transracial adoption should only occur after clearly documented evidence of unsuccessful same race adoption.

Myth #11: There are not sufficient numbers of same-race homes for African American children.

Response: A collaborative recruitment effort between the public and private foster care and adoption agencies with the African American community, families, and professionals, is essential. As of March 31, 1998, at least 110,000 children are in foster care with the goal of adoption. Twenty-nine percent are white, 59% are African American, and 10% are Hispanic [Maza 1998].

The overt barriers are evident in the costly fees established for adoption and in the screening out of potentially appropriate families in the home study process. Organizations that specialize in the recruitment of African American families and minority families experience excellent success in their recruitment efforts. These organizations are clearly ably to locate sufficient numbers of appropriate same race placement homes. (See Appendix E.)

Minimizing Barriers to Recruitment

In 1990, the North American Council on Adoptable Children (NACAC) conducted a survey of 64 private and 23 public child placing agencies in 25 states. Of the 64 private agencies, 17 specialized in minority placements (the placement of minority children with minority families). The survey highlighted policies and procedures most directly affecting the placement of minority children. A 42-item questionnaire was administered to executive directors, state adoption supervisors, program/unit heads, and case workers [Giles & Kroll 1991].

Eighty-three percent of the respondents said they were aware of organizational and/or institutional barriers preventing or discouraging families of color to adopt. Those identified most often are listed below:

- **Institutional/systemic racism.** Virtually all procedures and guidelines impacting standard agency adoption are developed from white middle-class perspectives.

- **Lack of people of color in managerial positions.** Boards of directors and agency heads remain predominantly white.

- **Fees.** Seventy-five percent of agencies surveyed said adoption fees are a barrier to minority families trying to adopt.

- **"Adoption as business" mentality/reality.** Heavy dependence upon fee income, coupled with the fact that supplies of healthy white infants are decreasing drastically, force many agencies to place transracially to ensure survival.

- **The historical tendency of communities of color toward "informal" adoption.** Potential adopters of color question the relevance of formalized adoption procedures, many times wondering why such procedures are needed at all.

- **Negative perceptions of agencies and their practices.** Families of color often possess negative perceptions of public and private agencies and their underlying motives.

- **Lack of minority staff.** Minority workers "in the trenches" are crucial in building trust among families of color. Consequently, their relative scarcity impedes minority families hoping to adopt.

- **Inflexible standards.** Insistence upon young, two-parent, materially endowed families eliminates many potentially viable minority homes.

- **General lack of recruitment activity and poor recruitment techniques.** Agencies are unable to set aside financial and human resources required for effective recruitment.

- **Poor publicity.** Communities of color remain largely unaware of the need for their services.

- **Fear of actual or potential litigation.** The ominous possibility of legal action by private citizens or the federal government leaves many agencies reluctant to recruit or pursue same-race placement and families.

According to the NACAC study, some agencies have "specialized" in placing children of a specific racial/cultural origin. These specialized agencies have had higher rates of same-race placements than "traditional" private agencies, placing 94% of their African American children and 66% of their Hispanic children in same-race homes, while traditional agencies placed 51% of their African American children and 30% of their Hispanic children with same-race families. NABSW cites this finding to dispel the myths that homes are not available in minority families, and to suggest that minority organizations have a high success rate of adoption and should be used more frequently [NABSW 1994].

NACAC's study proposes that there are lessons to be learned from agencies successfully placing large percentages of children in same-race families. The study highlights the following strategies and approaches for eliminating barriers to recruitment included:

- **Recruitment.** Recruitment must be ongoing and should include a wide variety of tools and techniques. Flexibility—screening families *in* rather than screening them *out*—is critical, as are cooperative arrangements with other organizations in the community.

- **Retention.** Staff must respond to potential adoptive parents quickly and openly and be available at times convenient for prospective parents, not vice versa.

- **The home study process.** Home studies must move away from an investigative style to an informative one. Flexibility and clear explanations should also play integral parts in culturally sensitive adoption studies.

- **Fees.** Adoption fees are perceived by respondents as having a dramatically negative impact on almost all prospective minority adopters. Agencies must commit to making fees reasonable for all, and must understand that the problems which families of color have with adoption fees are often as much attitudinal as financial. Professionals will need to provide thorough explanations distinguishing "fees for service" from the "buying of human flesh."

- **State involvement.** States must assume fiscal responsibility for costs of adoption if true commitments to same-race placement are to be made. States can assist private agencies by providing start-up funds for recruitment and retention programs, as well as supplying continuing support through ongoing purchase of service agreements.

Components of an Effective Recruitment Program

Research has identified components that are essential to developing an effective recruitment program. These components include information, intake, marketing, community, orientation/training/retention, and evaluation and assessment. Listed below are recommended guidelines for building and maintaining these components. The guidelines should be tailored to compliment your agency's goals and resources, as well as the community and prospective families' needs.

A consortium of agencies that specialize in African American adoptions has formed the National Center on Permanency for African American Children (see Appendix E). The following are guidelines they found to be successful in their recruitment programs.

Information

- Information and profiles about the children in need of homes:
  - Number of children
  - Number of sibling groups
  - Age distribution
  - Special needs of the child (types and number)
  - Length and number of placements
  - Permanency goal/plan (foster care or adoption)
  - Reunification or adoption: relative/nonrelative
  - Parents' status (i.e., termination of parental rights, in litigation)
  - Child's contact with parents/family
  - Reason for coming into care

- Information about the community:
  - Number of foster families and adoptive families
  - Estimated number of informal caregivers
  - Community's history of foster care and adoption (formal and informal)
  - Relationship of the community with social service institutions (i.e., protective services, children and youth agencies, family court, positive or negative)
  - Previous experience and exposure to foster care or adoption recruitment
  - Families' knowledge about foster care or adoption
  - Existing community or organizations (religious, political, social, educational)
  - Socioeconomic demographics about the community (i.e., employment status, income levels, household configurations)
- Information for distribution to the community and prospective families:
  - Information and profiles about the children in waiting
  - Types of homes the children need (i.e., nurturance, support, role models, attachments)
  - Qualifications for becoming prospective foster or adoptive parents (i.e., financial, legal, medical)
  - Orientation, preparation, approval, and selection process (i.e., timeframes, steps)
  - Supportive services (i.e., financial, legal, medical, emotional)
  - Benefits to the adoptive or foster family (i.e., emotional satisfaction)

- Benefit to the child (i.e., permanency, a family)
- Benefit to the community (i.e., not institutionalizing children, self-supporting, keeping children in community)
- Benefit to the adoption and foster care agency and organization (i.e., partnership, children with caring, protective, invested families)

Intake

- Processing phone and face-to-face or walk-in inquiries about foster care or adoptions (i.e., develop dialogue and protocols for putting calls on hold, number of transfers, providing bilingual staff)
- Provide information (i.e., initially verbally then written)
- Elicit interest and questions
- Initial screening of potential families for follow-up and outreach
- Arrange follow-up with potential parents (i.e., written information, appointment for initial orientation, phone contact, home visit)
- Get basic information from caller (i.e., name, phone number, how caller heard about program)
- If the person is not appropriate or qualified to be a prospective parent, identify other ways of helping or working with children (i.e., volunteer services, other agencies or careers)

Marketing

- Develop informational packs (i.e., mail outs, speakers, conferences, orientations)
- Implement market study and survey of the community

- Organize marketing plan (i.e., target population, educational forums, methods of disseminating information, contact sites, and outreach efforts)

- Organize marketing staff (i.e., speakers bureau, mail outs, phone call follow-ups)

- Manage and schedule requests for information, speakers, training, and educational activities

- Develop marketing strategies for recruiting potential parents

- Training and educating agency staff in their marketing roles (i.e., other foster or adoptive staff or case managers)

Community

- Identify and recruit key community members and organizations

- Recruit foster or adoptive parents

- Have committee involved in reviewing, developing, and decisionmaking regarding marketing plans and strategies

- Involve committee members in recruitment activities (i.e., sponsor or host activities, joint agency, and community activities)

- Compensate community members and organization (i.e., in-kind, monetary, service agreements)

- Involve committee in evaluating the recruitment, outcomes, accomplishments, and recommended actions

Orientation/Training/Retention

- Provide agency and community-based programs and training

- Assure accessibility

- Support families through the preparation, approval, and selection process

- Involve community advisory committee members in developing and evaluating the program

- Provide individual assistance with completed documentation

- Provide child care

- Offer transportation

- Offer reimbursements for expenses (i.e., child care, transportation)

- Follow-up and reschedule parents who are absent from training or orientation classes

- Remind parents of upcoming classes, training, or timetables for completing or providing documentation

Evaluation and Assessment

- Establish goals and measurable outcomes for each program component (i.e., intake, marketing, training/retention, community advisory, and evaluation)

- Provide ongoing evaluations monitoring and feedback (i.e., quarterly or monthly)

- Involve the prospective families and community advisory committee in the evaluation and feedback process (i.e., trainers, speakers, information, activities)

- Identify recruitment activities that produced the most response and interest

- Identify activities that were most frequently attended

- Identify sites that were most accessible for training and recruitment

- Identify organizations and groups that provided access to families, as well as groups needing to be approached

Retaining Families

Practitioners would do well to remember that their initial contact with the prospective family, community leader, or organization is the beginning of the retention process. Listed below are some recommendations for facilitating this process.

Elicit and Retain the Prospective Parents' Interests

How can you let prospective parents know that you are genuinely appreciative of their interest in transracial adoption or foster care? You can communicate that appreciation in many ways:

- Make the parents feel that you are first interested in them personally, then the children in care from their community.

- Communicate a respect for them, and for their family and community's interest in the well-being of children in care.

- Convey an appreciation for their interest and voluntary time to speak with or listen to you.

- Identify the need for partnership for the agency to accomplish its goals and mission.

- Identify their unique roles in providing the children with permanency in their community of racial and cultural origin.

Demystify the Preparation, Training Selection, and Approval Process

Clarifying the process is essential in retaining parents. Once the prospective parents meet the nonnegotiable standards and criteria, they must then be made to feel even more appreciated and needed by the program and children. Demystifying the process will help minimize the anxiety, fears, and self-doubt that may cause parents to avoid the tension by withdrawing from the process. Activities in this task include the following:

- Give families timetables for each phase of the process.

- Communicate your belief that they are capable of completing the process.

- Identify supports to help the family complete the process (i.e., contact person, individual attention).

- Provide visual aides that graphically identify the process, timetables, and requirements.

Develop Culturally Sensitive Programs, Support, and Training

It is imperative that parent training and preparation programs control for cultural bias. This is a complex issue that will challenge you and your agency's resources. Listed below are some recommended activities:

- Eliminate language barriers by having bilingual staff.

- Be sure that parents understand the terms, documents, language, and dialect being used in training.

- Provide same-race staff, foster, or adoptive parents as trainers and recruiters.

- Identify training or orientation locations and times that are accessible and compatible with the families and communities, routines, schedules, and activities.

Promote a Relationship of Mutual Education, Selection, and Approval

The families and community must also feel that your organization or agency seeks and needs their approval and selection as well. There are several ways that you can communicate this interdependence.

- Involve families and communities in the decisionmaking, planning, and evaluating of recruitment and training programs.

- Request the help of community organizations and families to educate staff about the community's resources and cultures and about ways that your agency can positively interact with the community.

- Elicit constructive criticism about past interactions between the community and your agency.

- Elicit feedback when racism, prejudice, or discrimination occurs in your agency's practices

- Identify a mechanism and structure for processing concerns or complaints with agencies, staff, or organizations.

Recruiting African American Families

The National Adoption Information Clearinghouse has provided guidelines and suggestions to agencies recruiting adoptive families in the African American community [NAIC 1998]. They have provided suggestions that address the development of materials for ethnic populations and media and nonmedia recruitment techniques.

Ethnic-, racial-, or culture-specific products should

- provide messages that include the language-diverse values and customs of the targeted community;

- provide printed materials that are concise, graphic, and pretested in the targeted community; and

- involve the community in the development and pretesting of products.

Working with the community should include

- learning what print and electronic media serve the minority community;

- providing the print media with articles about adoption, such as waiting children features, successful adoptions, the need for homes, and announcements about informational meetings;

- accessing the electronic media's public service announcements, interview shows, and news networks; and

- providing the electronic media with families for interviews, videotapes, photos, and printed materials about waiting children, the types of families needed, and how they apply and qualify.

Nonmedia recruitment techniques suggested by NAIC include the following:

- **Churches**: provide flyers, printed inserts in church bulletins, speakers for presentations and printed materials for announcements;

- **Fraternal and sorority organizations**: provide speakers, inserts, strategies for recruitment and community education;

- **Posters**: strategically placed in areas and locations frequented by the community;

- **Festival and cultural events**: organize speakers, booths, exhibits, and displays about adoption that elicit families to give their names, phone numbers, and addresses for follow-up and information; and

- **Transportation systems (used by the minority community)**: provide posters, graphics of children, adoptive families, and sources of information (i.e., phone numbers, places and dates of future meetings).

References

Gershenson, C. P. (1984, March). Community response to children free for adoption. *Child Welfare Research Notes*, *3*, 1-5.

Giles, T., & Kroll, J. (1991). *Barriers to same race placement*. St. Paul, MN: North American Council on Adoptable Children.

Hill, R. B. (1972). *The strength of Black families*. New York: Emerson Hall Publishers.

Ladner, J. A. (1977). *Mixed families: Adoptions across racial boundaries*. Garden City, NY: Doubleday, Anchor Press.

Maza, P. L. (1998). Personal communication with the author.

National Adoption Information Clearinghouse. (1998). *Adoptions and the African-American child: A guide for agencies.* Washington, DC: Author.

National Association of Black Social Workers. (1986). *Preserving Black families: Research and action beyond rhetoric.* New York: Author.

National Association of Black Social Workers. (1994). *Position statement: Preserving African American families.* Detroit, MI: Author.

U.S. Department of Health and Human Services, Administration of Children, Youth and Families. (1995). *Policy guidance on the use of race, color or national origin as consideration in adoption and foster care placements.* Washington, DC: Author.

Chapter Nine

Looking Ahead

The future presents major challenges for practitioners who are involved in transracial and/or transcultural adoptions and foster placements, such as the four listed below:

- the selection of foster and adoptive parents capable of parenting a child of a different culture or race,

- the preparation and training of parents and families for transracial adoption and foster care,

- the sensitizing and training of staff to provide pre- and postplacement services to transracial families, and

- the recruitment of families who reflect the racial and cultural diversity of children needing adoptive and foster homes.

The challenges of selecting families is further complicated by the need for agencies to comply with IEPA (see Appendix F for brief descriptions of relevant federal legislation). Any consideration of race, color, or national origin in foster or adoption placements must be "narrowly tailored" on an individualized basis for each child, in light of each prospective adoptive or foster parent's capacity to care for a child [DHHS 1997]. The future challenges for staff and agencies are to assess and determine if and how the prospective parent's capabilities are an advantage or disadvantage to the child.

The first objective is to explain why the parent's capacity to address racial and cultural issues is in the best interest of a child on a case-by-case basis. The second objective is to then determine the prospective's parents ability to meet and address the child's racial and cultural needs. These two objectives can be reached by allowing agencies to make the assessment and determination or by engaging families in a self-assessment and self-selection process. The self-assessment and self-selection appear to be the future trends for selecting prospective adoptive and foster parents. Professionals, agencies, and parent support groups will need to assist parents in understanding how and why addressing racial/cultural issues are in a child's best interest, in assessing their own ability to address these racial and/or cultural needs, and in determining if their fostering or adopting a child of a different race/culture is in the child's and their own best interests. This book has identified several self-assessment tools and guides that agencies may find useful (see Chapter 3).

Training and preparing prospective foster/adoptive parents before and after the placement of the child will also challenge professionals and agencies. The future trend is to provide training that incorporates orientation programs, preplacement classes, postplacement training, and ongoing support groups. This training may be either voluntary or mandatory as part of certification, licensing, and approval programs.

Providing pre- and postplacement services is another challenge. Organizations will need to develop services and service delivery models that are short-term, intermittent, and longitudinal. This book reviewed several service delivery models and approaches for consideration (see Chapter 6). Implementing these models requires that staff and organizations be culturally sensitive and competent to provide services (see Chapter 7).

The development of recruitment and retention programs of racially and culturally diverse families is also a major challenge at present—and in the future. The IEPA is the federal legislation that requires states to recruit potential foster and adoptive families who reflect the ethnic and racial diversity of children in need of out-of-home care [DHHS 1997].

Agencies and organizations will need to identify what barriers exist in their recruitment of diverse families, develop organizational strategies and structures for the recruitment of families, and identify and develop programs for the retention of families as well. The future goal for organizations and agencies is to maintain a constant source of available families for immediate consideration, who reflect a child's racial and cultural origin (see Chapter 8).

Recommendations for Research

As we work to improve public policies, case management, and professional practices, our efforts will need to be supported by research on the impact of transracial/transcultural adoption and foster care. Future research should focus on the outcomes of transracial placements and standards of practice and case management.

Research on the outcomes of transracial foster care and adoption should determine if these placements provide permanency for children by analyzing the percentage of disruptions, percentage of stable placements, and lengths of permanency in foster care and adoption. These findings should also be compared to same-race placements.

Practitioners should determine if there is any correlation between parenting style and training with the child's degree of racial and cultural identity to identify effective parenting techniques for transracial families. We must also continue to examine the degree of self-esteem and positive racial/cultural identity of children in transracial families (i.e., children and adult adoptees).

Other questions for future research to address include the following:

- What methods of training, assessment, and preparation of children and families were associated with permanent placements and adoptions? This finding should be compared to disruptions (foster care and adoptions).

- What policies, procedures, and methods of collaboration resulted in successful intercounty and interstate finalizations of adoptions?

- What are optimal caseloads and criteria for documenting effective reasonable efforts and time-limited reunification efforts?

- What is essential training for workers involved in transracial and transcultural adoptions and foster care?

- What judicial procedures and proceedings are effective models for ensuring timely permanency reviews, TPR petitions, finalization of adoptions, and involvement of foster or prospective adoptive parents in hearings?

- What are legally appropriate situations in which race and culture can be considered in decisions to place or not place a child in a transracial/cultural family?

References

U.S. Department of Health and Human Services, Administration on Children, Youth and Families [DHHS]. (1997). *Policy guidance on the Small Business Job Protection Act of 1996, Interethnic Adoption and Multiethnic Placement Act.* Washington, DC: Author.

A p p e n d i x   A

NACAC Self-Awareness Tool (excerpt)

Personal Motivations to Foster/Adopt

Caroline is a White social worker, her husband David is African American and a professor of history. Caroline has been in the field of social work nearly 16 years. Although she is now at the supervisory level and sees fewer clients, she remembers the numbers and types of children trapped within the system. Caroline and David's first adopted child was an infant, a victim of sexual abuse. Subsequent children adopted by the family had emotional and psychological conditions and were exposed to drugs during pregnancy.

In all, they have adopted three children within the United States. Christina, age 6, is African American; Timothy, age 7, is biracial; and Stephanie, age 9, is White. David loves each of the children that he and his wife have taken in. However, Caroline (not David) started the ball rolling on each of the three adoptions. "Caroline gets an idea into her head and there's no talking her out of it," David states. "As long as there are children in trouble and we have an extra bedroom, Caroline fills out an application to adopt another child. Caroline's mission is to do good on behalf of children!"

"I love children; it's as simple as that," Caroline explains. "I want each of our children to know a better life. In a way, I feel like I'm rescuing them."

• Caroline has a number of personal reasons to adopt children. Are her reasons appropriate? Can you identify with any of her reasons?

• It is clear from the story above that Caroline is involved in the adoption process. Describe David's role.

• Is it okay for Caroline to take an active role, while David's role is more passive? Explain.

• If Caroline or David were to adopt another child, they would need to tell the other children about their decision. If you were the parent, how would you do this?

• How do you suppose the newly adopted child will react to siblings of diverse backgrounds?

• Raising several children with different racial backgrounds may be quite difficult for Caroline and David. Think about and write down some of the challenges that they may face.

• What are some of the challenges that the children may face?

Exercise #1

Think about the reasons you want to adopt or foster a child of a different background. In some cases, there may be several reasons. Mark all that apply.

❑ You have an interracial marriage, so adopting a child of your spouse's (or your) race seems natural.

❑ You have adopted a child of a different race and want to add similar children to your family.

❐ You want children, but cannot get pregnant.

❐ In order to adopt a healthy infant, you need to adopt a child of another race or culture.

❐ You love children and can provide a good home.

❐ You feel you should adopt for moral or religious reasons.

❐ You feel sorry for children who were abused as youngsters.

❐ You want to foster a child because you have heard that going ahead with an adoption is easier if the child is already in your home as a foster child.

❐ Too many children are trapped in the foster care system, and you feel it is your duty to help.

❐ The system of adoption in the United States is too difficult, so an international placement is preferable.

❐ You have become attached to a particular foster child placed in your home.

❐ You think babies with darker complexions are cute.

❐ The agency told you that to adopt, you first had to become a foster parent.

❐ You love children and want to extend your family through adoption.

❐ You want to improve "race relations" by raising a child of another race or culture.

❐ You were once a foster child and want to give something back to another child.

Discussion

People have many different reasons for bringing a child into their home. Some of the examples listed on the previous page are appropriate reasons to foster or adopt transracially. Others are not. In the story above, Caroline adopted children out of love, but also because she felt she was doing something good for society. Although she and David provide a good home and care for the children, they have a responsibility to appreciate and celebrate each child's individual strengths and needs.

Statements like, "We're providing a better life," can be hurtful to a child—especially a child who has memories of biological relatives. Even children placed as infants can be hurt by these remarks. Children need to be loved for who they are, and shown over and over that their biological family and community of origin have not abandoned them. It is a tragedy when children mistakenly believe (or are told) that their community did not want them.

Further, the placement of a child should never happen simply because you feel sorry for a child or a child's background. Rather, it should happen because you truly want the child. If you bring a young person into your life because you pity them, you may unintentionally say or do things that tell the child that his/her culture is bad. Although you may not intend to paint a negative picture of your child's culture, the child may take your comments seriously. The child may feel self-conscious about his background and avoid people from his culture.

Some people believe it is their moral or religious duty to take in children from other countries who are less fortunate. The media often depict other countries as unpleasant places—dirty, violent, uncivilized, backward. If adoptive parents see only these messages, they may conclude that they are "rescuing the child" from a horrible life.

Young adults who were adopted from other countries urge prospective parents to visit the country ahead of time, before the paperwork is finalized. They encourage prospective parents to interact with the people, view the landscape, and experience the beauty of the country. Parents who go the extra mile to see the child's country in a positive light do a much better job of parenting that child.

Wanting a healthy infant is another reason parents have for adopting. When looking for a child of the same race, White parents realize that few of these children are available in the system today. In response, parents expand their search to children of other races or ethnicities. "We're open to any child," they tell their social worker. "We don't have any problems raising a child of color." The problem with these statements, however, is that the parents are only considering *their* abilities and *their* desires. Rather than asking, "Am I *willing* to raise a child of another background?" the more appropriate question is, *"Do I have what it takes* to raise a child of a different background?" There's a difference.

Parents who choose to foster or adopt out of love and respect for a child will ultimately be better suited for the role of parenting that child. Look again at your reasons to foster or adopt. Are they focused on yourself or the child? Are they based on respect or pity?

Home

Anna is a beautiful 8-year-old Latina girl who has been placed as a foster child in your African American family for the last year and a half. She has little contact with her biological family. As soon as Anna's parental rights are terminated, you hope to adopt her. One afternoon, an elderly neighbor, Thelma, stops by to drop off some things for an upcoming church fundraiser. Thelma is the "eyes and ears" of the neighborhood, and always seems to make *your* business her business. Your three children, including Anna, are playing in the room across the hall.

After a rather lengthy visit, Thelma stops by the front hallway on her way out to admire each of the newly hung school pictures. In her usual booming voice, she says, "What lovely photos. But why is Anna's here among all your family portraits? She's not a *real* member of your family." As soon as Thelma's words are spoken, the playful noises from across the hall are quieted. Every ear is listening for your response.

- How would you respond to Thelma's question?

- What do you suppose Anna is thinking when she hears her neighbor?

- Explain how you would feel if you were Anna.

- What are the most important things in your home that show a child she is welcome and part of the family?

- Describe the decorations on the walls of your home. What types of books do you display in your living or family room? Do they celebrate different cultures?

- What type of magazines do you have in your home? Name a few magazines written for and by your child's racial or cultural community.

- What types of food do you serve to your family? How willing would you be to prepare the cuisine of your child's background (for instance, fry bread, greens, kim chee, etc.)? Who can help you learn to cook the specialties of your child's culture?

- What bedtime stories will you read to your child? Do these books reflect your child's culture?

- Think about the music a child would hear in your home. Will that music help her learn about her culture of origin?

Discussion

Becoming a diverse family means a lot more than bringing the child home, unpacking toys, and setting up a bedroom. It means understanding what would make your child feel more comfortable in her surroundings and working to put her needs before yours.

As in Anna's story, displaying photos of the child clearly tells the child she is now a valued and important part of your family. But parents need to go further by showing and telling their children (and others) that their culture is valued and respected at home and in the family.

One important way to do this is to put yourself in awkward situations. For instance, many parents bring their families to special events in the child's community. If you and your Native American child attend a traditional tribal celebration together, your child sees his culture in action—he is an *insider*. If you are the only African American person there, you may receive some odd stares and feel uncomfortable at first. Your child sees that you are appreciating and learning about his culture, however. The benefits that children get from these experiences cannot be measured.

List several ways that you can face a personal challenge on behalf of your child.

-
-
-

Parents must also thing about the labels they use for their children. Be careful with the language you use to talk about your family. Here are some hints.

- **Birth children**. Preferred: birth child, biological, or simply use the child's first name. Discouraged: "This is my real child." "This is my natural child."

- **Adopted children**. Preferred: adopted, "my child," or simply use the child's first name. Discouraged: "my little China doll," "little brown bottom," "little Eskimo Pie."

- **Foster children**. Preferred: foster, or simply use the child's first name. Discouraged: "He's just a foster child." "He's not mine."

Reprinted from the *Self Awareness Tool* by Jeannette W. Bower, with permission from the North American Council on Adoptable Children (NACAC)

A p p e n d i x   B

Below the Surface:
Self-Assessment (excerpt)

Lifestyle

Where we live and who we know, things we do and places we frequent—these are the factors that comprise our lifestyle. Some of these questions can seem scary if you discover that your life is "Whiter" than you thought. The trust is that you, and especially your child, will have a much easier time.

Most families who adopt transracially are only beginning to assess their lives from the point of view of their child. Be honest with yourself. If you don't like your answers to these questions, your lifestyle is something you can choose to change.

• What is the racial makeup of your neighborhood?

❒ Mostly people of color

❒ Diverse, about half Caucasian, about half people of color

❒ Mostly Caucasian with some people of color

❒ All Caucasian

- If you adopted today, what other adopted children of color will your child get to meet?

  ❐ None

  ❐ Some, because I participate in a support/parent group

  ❐ Some, because I know other families with adopted children

  ❐ Many, because I have sought out adoptive families

- What other adults of color will your child know who are adopted?

  ❐ None

  ❐ A few I happen to know

  ❐ A few, because I have sought out adult role models for my child

  ❐ Many, because I have sought out adoptive families

- How often and under what circumstance do you interact with people of other races?

  ❐ All the time—with good friends, in my home and theirs, in my neighborhood, at church, at work, and in professional contexts

  ❐ At work and in professional contexts, traveling to new places

  ❐ I don't have much opportunity, although I am open to it

  ❐ Almost never; I would feel uncomfortable initiating contact

Knowledge

How much do you really know about your child's heritage? Most of us learn nothing in school about the history or contributions of people of color in America, and, consequently, we generally don't know much. Don't get discouraged here—get energized.

There are whole new worlds you can learn about and help your child discover. The path to future learning and growth can be lit by recognizing what you know and don't know. Knowledge is something you can acquire by reading, watching films, and talking with and listening to experts, just to name a few. If you choose do to so, you can learn about anything you want to, at your own pace, and in your own space.

- At what age do you think children notice racial differences?

  ❐ 2 to 3 years old

  ❐ 4 to 6 years old

  ❐ 7 to 10 years old

- Why do you think children notice racial differences?

  ❐ Because they are observant and curious about the world

  ❐ Children notice racial differences because of bias based on race

  ❐ Children have to be taught to notice racial differences

- How old do you think your children will be when they first ask about racial differences?

  ❐ 2 to 3 years old

  ❐ 8 to 10 years old

  ❐ I don't think they will ask too many questions

- When do you imagine the subject of race will first come up with a transracially adopted child?

  ❐ When she notices difference between her parents and herself

  ❐ When someone points out differences between her parents and herself (like at school).

❐ When she is old enough to read or hear about racism from strangers, books, movies of the media.

Reprinted from *Below the Surface*, a self-assessment guide for adoptive parents considering adoption across racial and cultural limes. Authors are Beth Hall and Gail Steinberg. Reprinted with permission from Pact: An Adoption Alliance.

A p p e n d i x   C

An Insider's Guide to
Transracial Adoption (excerpt)

Objective

Prospective parents will consider for themselves if their lifestyle, attitude, education, and temperament support transracial adoption. Those who determine that it does will understand the complexities that come with this form of family life. Those who determine that it does not will feel supported and positive about withdrawing from this form of adoption plan.

Trainer Preparation/Concepts to Understand

Parenting any child is challenging. Parenting an adopted child adds a second layer of complexity to family life. Parenting a child of a different race than your own creates yet a further layer of complexity. Not everyone can feel comfortable with this form of parenting. If the prospective parents by temperament seek to avoid attention, yearn to fit in rather than stand out, and manage life best through a process of simplifying rather than multiplying things that must be handled, they will be immensely frustrated with the life changes of transracial adoption, which have inherent within them the opposites of each of these patterns.

As personality traits that influence our comfort with these things are hard-wired, they are not likely to change. Attitude, lifestyle, and education can be changed by those who pursue this route to adoption and most often must be. This requires strong commitment to the hard work of making significant changes to understanding racism and in particular seeing our own racist attitudes that we are not aware of, but which are hard to avoid in a society that favors whites. It also requires changing our lifestyles to diversify the people we interact with and building new, strong links across lines of color, and learning all that none of us has been taught in school about the history, culture, achievements, traditions, etc., of people of our child's race. No one who feels discomfort considering changes should pursue this path. The prospective parent knows him- or herself better than the worker can. We are limited to the information they provide, collected in a short timeframe, rather than over a lifetime. The goal is to make it safe for the prospective parents to apply their knowledge of self to the predictable challenges that come with choosing transracial adoption to make an informed decision about their own suitability for the task.

Note: These are our general suggestions for pre- and postadoption workshop series. You know best the needs and interests of the group you are planning for. Every module is appropriate for any transracial adoptive or foster parent.

Pre-Adopt Series Planner

3-Session Series
1. Visible differences
2. Below the surface
3. Racial identify

5-Session Series
1. Visible differences
2. Below the surface
3. Racial identify
4. Counterintuitive parenting
5. Seeking diversity

12-Session Series
1. Visible differences
2. Below the surface
3. Racial identify
4. Counterintuitive parenting
5. Prepare, don't protect
6. Seeking diversity
7. Birth parents
8. Mainstreaming
9. Facing the issues
10. How to connect
11. Strategies for dealing with racism
12. Conclusions

Post-Adopt Series Planner

3-Session Series

1. Visible differences
2. How to connect
3. Talking with children about racism

5-Session Series

1. Visible differences
2. Prepare, don't protect
3. Birth parents
4. How to connect
5. Talking with children about racism

10-Session Series

1. Visible differences
2. Prepare, don't protect
3. Birth parents
4. How to connect
5. Talking with children about racism
6. Strategies for dealing with racism
7. Mainstreaming
8. What are the rules
9. Skill mastery
10. Personalizing culture

Reprinted from the *Trainer's Guide* by Gail Steinberg and Beth Hall with permission from Pact: An Adoption Alliance.

A p p e n d i x D

NACAC Training Curriculum (excerpt)

Cultural Identity

Objectives:

Purpose: To discuss the importance of a child's identity with his culture or community of origin.

Goal: To educate parents on ways to integrate the child's background into their family.

Results: Parents will begin to actively seek out their child's community or culture of origin, and integrate it into the family's daily life.

Agenda and Timeline

Overview of Session	5 min
Minilecture	10 min
Exercise #1	20 min
Exercise #2	20 min
Break	10 min
Role Play	30 min
Wrap Up	5 min
TOTAL	1 hours 40 min

Materials

- Overhead projector and visual aids (transparencies)
- Chalkboard and chalk or flip chart and several colored markers
- Copies of handouts and exercises

Notes to the Trainer

Parents have an important role to play in the development of their child's cultural identity. We need to start early by enforcing positive images of the child's culture or community of origin. At times, we may be influenced by others and think about taking the easy way out by avoiding culture all together. For the child's sake, we must work every day to show the child the beauty of his culture or community. The child's self-esteem and coping skills are dependent upon our success.

Racism

Objectives

Purpose: To discuss ways children of color and their families will experience discrimination and racism during their lives.

Goal: To educate parents about the ways that racism influences a child's sense of identity.

Results: Parents will begin to think about and develop strategies for preparing their family for racism and its effects.

Agenda and Timeline

Overview of Session	5 min
Minilecture	10 min
Exercise #1	20 min
Exercise #2	20 min
Break	10 min
Panel Discussion	90 min
Wrap Up	5 min
TOTAL	2 hours 40 min

Materials

- Overhead projector and visual aids (transparencies)
- Chalkboard and chalk *or* flip chart and several colored markers
- Copies of handouts and exercises

Note: Work with the agency to organize a panel discussion of five to eight young adults who were raised in families of a different race or culture.

Notes to the Trainer

This may likely be a difficult discussion for some parents. We realize that some people may not recognize that we live in a race-conscious society or that people are discriminated against because of their race, the color of their skin, the inflection in their voice, the texture of their hair, or any other number of reasons.

Reprinted from the *Training Curriculum* by Jeanette W. Bower with permission from the North American Council on Adoptable Children.

A p p e n d i x E

Resources

Parent Support Groups

Adoption with Wisdom and Honesty
  1333 Ranch Road
  McPherson, KS 67460
  716/924–5295

Association of Korean Adoptees
  1208 N. Brand Boulevard
  Glendale, CA 91202
  818/547–4945

Bay Area Association of Transracial Adoptees
  5500 MacArthur Boulevard
  Oakland, CA 94613
  510/430–3163

The Biracial Family Network
  P.O. Box 3214
  Chicago, IL 60654–0214
  773/288–3044

Families with Children Adopted from Bulgaria
7933 NE 124th Street
Kirkland, WA 198034
206/823–8018

Families with Children Adopted from China
P.O. Box 93271
Phoenix, AZ 85070–3271
602/893–0553

Families with Children Adopted from India
2031 216th Place, NE
Redmond, WA 98053
205/868–6259

Guatemalan North American Adoptive Families
2810 1st Avenue, North
Seattle, WA 91809
206/285–6254

Heritage for Black Children
4908 Center Lane
Orlando, FL 32808
407/299–5770

Latin American Parents Association
P.O. Box 523
Unionvillve, CT 06085–0523
203/270–1424

Native American Adoption Resource Exchange Council
Three Rivers American Indian Center
120 Charles Street
Pittsburgh, PA 15238
412/782–4457

Organizations and Agencies

The Adoption Exchange
925 South Niagara Street, Suite 100
Denver, CO 80224
303/333–0845
Fax: 303/320–5434

Adoptive Families of America
2309 Como Avenue
St. Paul, MN 55108
651/645–9950 or 800/372–2200
Fax: 651/645–0055

Asian American Curriculum Project, Inc.
234 Main Street
P.O. Box 1587
San Mato, CA 94401
650/343–9408
Fax: 650/343–6711

Center of Family Connections
P.O. Box 383246
Cambridge, MA 02238–3246
617/547–0909
Fax: 617/497–5952

Guide to Multicultural Resources
Praxis Publications, Inc.
P.O. Box 9809
Madison, WI 53715
606/244–5033

Institute for Black Parenting
9920 La Cienga Boulevard, Suite 806
Inglewood, CA 90301
310/348–1400
Fax: 310/215–3325

Joint Council on International Children's Services
7 Chenerly Circle
Chenerly, MD 20785–3040
301/322–1906
Fax: 301/322–3425

National Adoption Center on Permanency for African American Children
Howard University – School of Social Work
601 Howard Place, NW
Washington, DC 20059
202/806–7300
Fax: 202/387–4309

National Consortium on Permanency for Waiting Children
1821 University Avenue, N–263
St. Paul, MN 55104
888/840–4048

Northwest Indian Child Welfare Institute
Parry Center for Children
3415 S.E. Powell Boulevard
Portland, OR 97202
503/222–4044
Fax: 503/222–4007

Spaulding for Children
16250 Northland Drive, Suite 120
Southfield, MI 48075
810/443–7080
Fax: 810/443–7099

Welcome House
P.O. Box 181
Repkasie, PA 18944
215/249–0100
Fax: 215/249–9651

Magazines and Catalogs

Biracial Child Magazine
   P.O. Box 12048
   Atlanta, GA 30355
   404/350–7877

Children's Book Press (catalogs)
   246 First Street, Suite 101
   San Francisco, CA 94105
   415/995–2200
   Fax: 415/995–2222

Interrace Magazine
   P.O. Box 12048
   Atlanta, GA 30355
   404/350–7877

Korean Quarterly
   P.O. Box 6789
   St. Paul, MN 55106
   651/771–8164

Multicultural Review
   Greenwood Publishing Group
   88 Post Road West, P.O. Box 5007
   West Port, CT 06881–5007
   800/225–5800
   Fax: 203/221–1087

National Association for the Education of Young Children (catalogs)
   1509 16th Street NW
   Washington, DC 20036–1426
   202/232–8777
   Fax: 202/328–1846

The Roundtable
Spaulding for Children
16250 Northland Drive, Suite 120
810/443–7080
Fax: 810/443–7099

Tapestry Books (catalog)
P.O. Box 359
Ringues, NJ 08551–0359
800/765–2367
Fax: 908/788–2999

Websites

Adoption Network: http://www.adoption.org

Adoption Resources: http://www.adopting.com

Adoptive Families Of America: http://www.adoptivefam.org

Association of Black Social Workers: http://ww.greatinfo.com/absw/tap.html

Child Welfare League of America: http://www.cwla.org

Children's Bureau, Administration of Children and Family Department of Health and Human Services: http://www.acf.dhhs.gov/programs/cb/

Dave Thomas Foundation for Adoption: http://www.wendys.com/community/adoption/foundation.html

International and Transracial Adoptions: http://www.cyfc.umn.edu/adoptinfo/international.html

National Adoption Information Clearinghouse: http://www.calib.com/naic

North American Council on Adoptable Children: http://members.aol.com/nacac

Pact: An Adoption Alliance: http://www.pactadopt.org

Spaulding for Children: http://www.spaulding.org

Transracial and Transcultural Adoption: http://www.rainbowkids.com

The Transracial Group: http://www.transracial–adoption.org

Videos

Children's Home Society of Minnesota
"The Korean Teen Experience"
651/646–6393
2230 Como Avenue
St. Paul, MN 55108

National Resource Center for Special Needs Adoption
"Working with Afro–American Families"
313/375–8693
P.O. Box 337
Chelsea, MI 48118

New York State Coalition for Children
"Struggles for Identity: Issues in Transracial Adoptions"
607/272–4242
PhotoSynthesis
418 N. Tioga Street
Ithaca, NY 14850

North Bay Adoptions
"Visible Differences: Transracial Parenting
Through Adoptions"
707/570–2940
862 Third Street
Santa Rosa, CA 95404

Spaulding for Children
"Asian/Asia American Culture"
"Black Boys Are Wonderful"
"Hispanic/Latino Culture"
"Native American Culture"
"Making a Difference"
810/443–7080
162 South Northland Drive
Southfield, MI 48075

Books for Parents

Our Native American Child
Carolyn F. McPherson
Available through Spaulding for Children; 810/443–7080

Transracial Adoptive Parenting: A Black/White Community Issue
Al Stumph and Leona Neal
Available through Haskett–Neal; 518/392–5848

White Privilege: Unpacking the Invisible Knapsack
P. McIntosh
Available through Pact Press; 415/221–6957

Korea – New True Books
Available through Adoptive Families of America; 651/645–9955

Baby Face
Gail Johnson
Available through Adoptive Families of America; 651/645–9955

The Best of Adopted Child: Ethnic and Cultural Identity
Lois Melina
Available through Pact Press; 415/221–6957

Raising Adopted Children
Lois Melina
Available through Harper Perennial

Transracial Adoption: Children and Parents Speak
by Constance Pohl and Kathy Harris

Dounia
(A Child's Feelings About Interracial Adoption)
by Natacha Karvoskaia Zidrou

Our Children from Latin America
by Laurel Strassberger

A World of Love
by Maggie Francis Conroy

"Are Those Kids Yours?" American Families with Children Adopted from Other Countries
by Cheri Register

Oriental Children in American Homes: How Do They Adjust?
by Frances M. Koh

Butterflies in the Wind: Spanish/Indian Children with White Parents
by Jean Nelson–Erichhsen and Heino R. Erichsen

International Adoption: Sensitive Advice for Prospective Parents
by Jean Knoll and Mary–Kate Murphy

Gift Children: A Story of Race, Family and Adoption in a Divided America
by J. Douglas Bates

Outer Search/Inner Journey
by Peter Dodds

Adopted from Asia: How It Feels to Grow Up in America
by Frances M. Koh

Agencies Specializing in African American Adoptions

African–American Adoption & Permanency Planning Agency (AAAPPA)

Jacqueline B. Kidd, President and CEO
1821 University Avenue, N–263
St. Paul, MN 55104–2803
651/659–0460
Fax: 651/644–5306
http://www.aaappa.org
E–mail: aaappa@aaappa.org

Another Choice for Black Children

Ruth Amerson, Executive Director
5736 North Tyron Street, Suite 220
Charlotte, NC 28213
704/599–7749
Fax: 704/599–7752
E–mail: another@bellsouth.net

Coordinators/2

C. Lynne Edwards, Executive Director
5204 Patterson Avenue, Suite B
Richmond, VA 23266
804/288–7595
Fax: 804/288–7599
http://www.members.aol.com/c2adop
E–mail: c2adopt@aol/com

Family and Child Services

Homes for Black Children
Mae Best, Director
929 L Street, NW
Washington, DC 2001
202/289–1510
Fax: 202/371–0863
E–mail: fesmis@richochet.net

Homes for Black Children
Sydney Duncan, President and Clinical Director
511 E. Larned
Detroit, MI
313/961–4777

Howard University School of Social Work
Holy Cross Hall, 3rd Floor
Washington, DC 20059
202/806–7324
Fax: 202/387–4309
E–Mail: NCPWC@NCPWC.org
http://www.nepwe,org

Institute for Black Parenting
Zena Oglesby, Executive Director
9920 La Cienega Boulevard, Suite 806
Inglewood, CA 90301
310/348–1400
Fax: 310/215–3325

Mississippi Families for Kids
Linda West, Executive Director
620 N. Satte Street, Suite #304
Jackson, MN 39202
601/360–0591

Roots
Tom Oliver, Executive Director
1777 Phoenix Parkway, Suite 108
Atlanta, GA 30349
770/907–7770
Fax: 770/907–7726
E–mail: radopt@bellsouth.net

Federally Funded Programs

The North American Council on Adoptable Children (NACAC)

907 Raymond Avenue, Suite 106

St. Paul, MN 55114–1149

651/644–3036

Fax: 651/644–9848

Resource Materials

Training Curriculum by Jeannette W. Bower

Self–Awareness by Jeannette W. Bower

Parenting Resource Manual by Jeannette W. Bower and Susan Cunningham

Pact: An Adoption Alliance

3450 Sacramento Street, Suite 239

San Francisco, CA 94118

415/221–6957

Fax: 510/482–2089

Resource Materials

The Booksource: More than 1,000 referrals to books for children and adults related to adoption and race with descriptions of the book and a brief synopsis

Transracial Adoption Parent Support (TAPS): telephone line offering peer support to transracial and transcultural adoptive families at 415/451–8277 (call returned within 24 hours)

A Safe Awareness Guide by Gail Steinberg and Beth Hall

Visible Difference: a videotape examining transracial adoptions

Intentional Families, Interwoven Cultures: an audiocassette addressing the challenges of transracial adoptions

The Best of *Adopted Child*: Ethnic and Cultural Identity by Lois Melina

New York State Citizen's Coalition for Children, Inc.

306 East State Street, Suite 220

Ithaca, NY 14850

607/272–0034

Fax: 607272–0035

Resource Materials

<u>Struggles for Identity: Issues in transracial Adoption,</u> designed to inform adoptive and foster parents and professionals about the needs of children from different raced and cultural

Information and referral services to adoptive/foster parents and professionals about the needs of children from different races and cultures

A p p e n d i x   F
Federal Legislation

Multiethnic Placement Act

The Multiethnic Placement Act (MEPA) (P. L. 108-382), signed into law by President Clinton in October 1994, is designed to prevent discrimination in the placement of children on the basis of race, color, or national origin; facilitate the diligent recruitment of foster and adoptive parents; and to increase the number of children who are adopted. MEPA was designed to help children in foster care who are awaiting adoption—especially those children who are harder to place, such as children of color.

As originally adopted, the statute

- prohibited states or public and private foster care and adoption agencies that receive federal funds from delaying or denying the placement of any child solely on the basis of race, color, or national origin.

- permitted an agency to consider both a child's cultural, racial, and ethnic background and the capacity of the foster or adoptive parents to meet the needs of a child of a specific background, as one of a number of factors used in determining whether a placement is in the child's best interests.

- required agencies to provide for the diligent recruitment of potential foster and adoptive families that reflect the ethnic and racial diversity of children in the state for whom foster and adoptive homes are needed.

Interethnic Adoption Provisions of 1996

On August 20, 1996, President Clinton signed the Small Business Job Protection Act (P. L. 104-188). Section 1808 of the act, entitled Removal of Barriers to Interethnic Adoption (IEP), amended MEPA by strengthening the prohibition against discrimination in adoption or foster care placements. It does this by repealing Section 553 of MEPA, which has the effect of removing from the statute the language:

> Permissible Consideration—An agency or entity [which receives federal assistance] may consider the cultural, ethnic, or racial background of the child and the capacity of the prospective foster or adoptive parents to meet the needs of a child of such background as one of a number of factors used to determine the best interests of a child.

The Interethnic Adoption Provisions maintain a prohibition against delaying or denying the placement of a child for adoption or foster care on the basis of race, color, or national origin of the adoptive or foster parent, or the child involved, and also maintains the requirement that states diligently recruit potential foster and adoptive families who reflect the ethnic and racial diversity of children in need of care.

The U.S. Department of Health and Human Services issued an information memorandum to states on May 11, 1998, stating that public agencies may not routinely consider race, national origin, and ethnicity in making placement decisions.

The Adoption and Safe Families Act

On November 19, 1997, President Clinton signed into law the Adoption and Safe Families act of 1997 (P.L. 105-89), which was designed to promote adoption and support families. Several of the most important adoption provisions include the following:

- circumstances in which reasonable efforts are not required before filing termination of parental rights (TPR) petitions;

- concurrent planning and efforts to place a child for adoption, concurrently with efforts to preserve or reunify a family;

- family reunification services limited to 15 months, beginning on the date of a child's removal from his or her home;

- an initial permanency hearing being held 12 months (formerly 18 months) from the date a child enters foster care;

- TPR filing for children in foster care 15 of the last 22 months (except in certain circumstances);

- notices served to foster parents, relatives, or preadoptive parents, giving them an opportunity to voice their opinions;

- fiscal incentives for states that increase their rates and number of adoptions;

- the removal of obstacles to intercounty and state adoptions; and

- incentives in the form of health coverage to children with special needs.

Bibliography

Abramovitz, M. (1991). Living in a racially-mixed family: A question of attitude. *OURS, 24*, 27.

Ahn, H. N. (1989). *Identity development in Korean adolescent adoptees: Eriksonian ego identity and racially ethnic identity.* Berkeley, CA: University of California School of Social Welfare.

Barnes, D. (1992). Building a family: One color at a time. *AdoptNet, 3*, 7-8.

Bartholet, E. (1993). *Family bonds: Adoption and the politics of parenting.* Boston: Houghton Mifflin Company.

Bates, J. D. (1993). *Gift children: A story of race, family and adoption in a divided America.* New York: Ticknor & Fields.

Berbaum, M., & Moreland, R. (1985) Intellectual development within transracial adoptive families: Retesting the confluence model. *Child Development, 56*, 206-216.

Camblin, L., & Milgram, J. (1982). Reflections on transracial adoptions: Two fathers' perspectives. *Social Work, 27*, 535.

Caldwell-Hopper, K. (1991). Adopting across lines of color. *OURS, 24*, 23-25.

Center for Early Education and Development. (1991). Baby D: What are the child development issues. *Fact, find* (3). Minneapolis, MN: Author.

Darder, E. (1991). Biracial and proud! *F.A.C.E Facts, 14*, 10-11.

Families Adopting Children Everywhere. (1991). How to keep racism from defeating your child. *F.A.C.E. Facts, 14*, 22.

Fahlberg, V. (1985). *Attachment and separation.* London: British Agencies for Adoption and Fostering.

Fahlberg, V. (1988). *Fitting the pieces together.* London: British Agencies for Adoption and Fostering.

Feigelman, W., & Silverman, A. (1983). *Chosen children: New patterns of adoptive relationships.* New York: Praeger Publishers.

Flango, V. E., & Flango, C. R. (1993). Adoption statistics by state. *Child Welfare, 72*, 311-319.

Frey, S. (1991). Interracial families. *AdoptNet, 3*, 40-41, 46.

Hornyak, C. (1990). Therapy techniques for families of transracial adoption. *Adoption Therapist, 1*, 2-3.

Jones, C., & Else, J. (1979). Racial and cultural issues in adoption. *Child Welfare, 62*, 374.

McFarlane, J. (1992). Building self-esteem in children and teenagers of color. *OURS, 5*, 28-33.

McFarlane, J. (1992). Self-esteem in children of color: Developmental, adoption, and racial issues. *OURS, 25*, 24-29.

McRoy, R. G. (1986). Racial identity issues of mixed race children: Implication for school social workers. *Social Work in Education, 8*, 164-174.

McRoy, R. G. (1990). Assessing cultural and racial identity. In S. Logan, E. Freeman, & R. G. McRoy (Eds.), *Social work practice with Black families.* White Plains, NY: Longham, Inc.

McRoy, R. G. (1990). An organizational dilemma: The case of transracial adoptions. *Journal of Applied Behavioral Science, 25*, 145-160.

McRoy, R., Zurcher, L., Lauderdale, M., & Anderson, R. (1982). Self-esteem and racial identity in transracial and inracial adoptees. *Social Work, 27*, 522-35.

McRoy, R. G., Zurcher, L. A., Lauderdale, M., & Anderson, R. E. (1984). The identity of transracial adoptees. *Social Casework, 65*, 34-39.

Meer, J. (1986). Adopting the melting pot. *Psychology Today, 20*, 17.

Melina, L. (1988). Cultural identity goes beyond ethnic foods, dolls. *Adopted Child, 7*, 1-4.

Melina, L. (1994). Transracial adoptees can develop racial identity, coping strategies. *Adopted Child, 13*, 1-4.

Moore, E. (1986). Family socialization and the IQ test performance of traditionally and transracially adopted Black children. *Developmental Psychology, 22*, 317-26.

Nelson-Erichsen, J., & Erichson, H. R. (1992). *Butterflies in the wind: Spanish/Indian children with White parents.* The Woodlands, TX: Los Niños International Adoption Center.

O'Rourke, L., Hubbell, R., Goolsby, S., & Smith, D. (1994). *Intercounty adoption* (rev. ed.). Rockville, MD: National Adoption Information Clearinghouse.

Parkas, C., & Stevenson-Hinde. (Eds.). (1982). *The place of attachment in human behavior.* New York: Basic Books.

Pederson, J. (1992). Traveling to your child's country of origin. *OURS, 25*, 40-42.

Pohl C., & Harris, K. (1992). *Transracial adoption: Children and parents speak.* New York: Franklin Watts.

Raible, J. (1990, Summer). Continuing the dialogue on transracial adoption. *Adoptalk, 5.*

Register, C. (1991). *Are those kids yours? American families with children adopted from other countries.* New York: Free Press.

Register, C. (1994). Are White people colorless? *OURS, 27*, 32-24.

Phinney, J. S., & Ritherman, M. J. (1987). *Children's ethnic socialization.* Beverly Hills, CA: Sage.

Shireman, J. F., & Johnson, P. R. (1986). A longitudinal study of Black adoptions: Single parent, transracial and traditional. *Social Work, 31*, 172-6.

Simon, R., & Alstein, H. (1977). *Transracial adoption*. New York: John Wiley and Sons.

Simon, R., & Alstein, H. (1982). *Adoption, race and identity: From infancy through adolescence.* New York: Praeger.

Singer, L., Brodzinsky, D., & Ramsay, D. (1985). Mother-infant attachment in adoptive families. *Child Development, 56,* 1543-51.

Van Gulden, H. (1992). *Attachment and bonding in adoptive families.* Workshop at Families Adopting Children Everywhere (F.A.C.E.) Conference, Towson, Maryland, May 1992.

Watkins, K. (1987). *Parent-child attachment.* New York: Garland Publishing.

Williams, J., & Morland, J. K. (1976). *Race, color and the young child.* Chapel Hill, NC: The University of North Carolina Press.

About the Author

Joseph Crumbley received his Masters and Doctorate in Social Work from the University of Pennsylvania. He is in private practice as a consultant and family therapist. His areas of specialization include pre- and postadoptive therapy, chemical dependency, couples therapy, and physical and sexual abuse. His services include case consultation, training, grantmanship, program evaluation, and organizational development. His most recent areas of concentration have been kinship care and transracial adoptions.

In the area of transracial adoptions, he has been a consultant to Los Angeles County Children and Youth Services, the New Jersey Adoption Resource Centers, the Black Adoption Consortium, and the Pennsylvania Legislative Task Force on the Multiethnic Placement Act. Presentations and workshops on the transracial adoptions have included the 1992, '93, '94, '95, '96 and '97 North American Conference on Adoptable Children (NACAC), the U.S. Department of Health and Human Services (HHS) 1994 and '85 Conferences on Minority Children, and the "Montel Williams Show" on transracial adoptions.

In the area of kinship care, Dr. Crumbley has been a consultant to the Los Angeles Kinship Care Program, the Child Welfare Institute, the Child Welfare League of America (CWLA), the Spaulding Center, and the Philadelphia Society's Kinship Care Program. He has made presentations at the Los Angeles County Kinship Care Conference, the National Association of Foster Parents Conference, HHS Fourth Annual Child Welfare Conference, CWLA Kinship Care Conference and the "Montel Williams Show" on kinship care.

Dr. Crumbley coauthored a book with Robert Little entitled *Kinship Care: Relatives Raising Children* published by the Child Welfare League of America. He has also completed a series of four audiovisual training tapes for parents and professionals on transracial adoptions. For more information about the author, consult his website www.drcrumbley.com.